Train Your Brain

Train
Your Brain

The Complete
Mental Workout for a
Fit and Agile Mind

By Joel Levy

BARNES
& NOBLE

NEW YORK

Contents

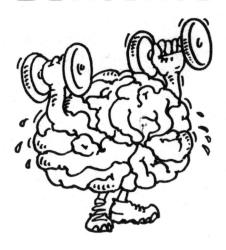

"Anyone who makes a distinction between games and learning doesn't know the first thing about either."
MARSHALL MCLUHAN

Introduction

Mental workouts

The humble crossword is rapidly becoming a celebrity, alongside other A-listers of the puzzle world, such as Sudoku and Kakuro. After decades spent languishing in the comparative obscurity of puzzle pages and specialty publications, brainteasers have suddenly invaded center spreads and front pages. What has propelled such previously unassuming pastimes into the spotlight?

It turns out that puzzles are not simply "a bit of fun" or a diverting amusement–they are actually good for you, providing the cognitive (thinking and related activities) equivalent of physical exercise. There is a growing body of evidence that mental exercise of the sort offered by brainteasers and puzzles can benefit you in two ways: braintenance and cognitive boosting.

Braintenance

Braintenance is the ungainly but popular term increasingly used to describe the idea of maintaining your brain so that it retains its functions and health and so that the aging process is slowed. Braintenance may even help to slow or prevent the onset of dementia and Alzheimer's disease.

Health experts have long suspected that following a healthy lifestyle–taking regular cardiovascular exercise, following a low-fat diet, avoiding smoking and drinking, and reducing stress, helps to protect against strokes and to maintain a healthy blood supply to the brain. But a number of studies, including a particularly impressive long-term study into the cognitive and brain health of a group of nuns in Mankato, Minnesota, have shown that this kind of healthy lifestyle, in addition to some other factors, can make the difference between cognitive decline and dementia on the one hand, and a fully active, sharp mind that lasts into extreme old age, on the other.

7

The "other factors," identified by David Snowdon of the Sanders-Brown Center on Aging at the University of Kentucky in Lexington, in his "Mankato Nun Study," included a positive attitude to life, a degree of spirituality, a good supply of folic acid, and a regular program of cognitive exercise in the form of adult education (lifelong learning), wide reading, stimulating discussion, and a predilection for crosswords, puzzles, and other such pastimes.

Cognitive boosting

More controversial, until recently, has been the idea that you could not only maintain your cognitive function but even boost it. Most experts think that IQ is mainly determined by genes and environmental factors in early life (for example, nutrition during infancy), that, in turn, means that by adulthood your IQ is largely set. But several studies have shown that specific mental exercises can produce measurable changes in the brain which can be observed with brain scans. For instance, a 2005 study from the University of Kentucky in Lexington suggests that regular meditation actually thickens the cortex (the outer layer of the brain) in the regions associated with attention and sensory processing.

Can mental exercise actually boost performance? There's little doubt that familiarity with the material and practice on sample questions can improve your performance on intelligence tests, but recent research goes even further. According to an experiment by the BBC conducted in March 2006, a program of simple mental exercise (which included puzzles and brainteasers) followed for just one week was enough to boost IQ by up to 40 percent in some subjects!

Most experts would probably steer shy of making such extravagant claims, but the point is that there is a growing acceptance that mental exercise really works and should be as much a part of a healthy lifestyle as a good diet and physical exercise.

Train your brain

This book is intended to introduce you to a range of mental exercises that could help you to achieve both braintenance and cognitive boosting. It presents mental challenges and exercises that seek to test, tease, and expand your abilities in a range of areas, including the main abilities or aptitudes that fall under the more general heading of "intelligence": mental speed, verbal aptitude (ability with words and language), numerical aptitude (ability with numbers and mathematical reasoning), spatial aptitude (ability to think in terms of space, form, shape, and pattern), logical aptitude (ability to use logical thinking), creative thinking (especially as applied to problem solving), and memory (that is involved in most, if not all, of the other abilities). There are specific chapters on two of the most popular forms of everyday mental exercise, Sudoku and Kakuro puzzles, that are powerful and fun tools to exercise logical aptitude.

These are not the only mental abilities, nor even the only forms of intelligence. Abilities or traits such as wisdom, knowledge/ learning, or emotional intelligence are harder to practice and do not lend themselves to puzzles, games, and brainteasers in the same fashion, and so are not dealt with in this book.

Cross training

The challenges, teasers, puzzles, games, and exercises come in a wide variety of formats. For instance, you'll find questions like those you might encounter in an IQ test and puzzles like the ones you might see in a newspaper. This reflects the varied nature of the abilities and aptitudes dealt with. Adapting to new and varied mental challenges makes mental exercise more effective, just as cross-training makes physical exercise more effective. Work through the whole book and you'll not only be better equipped to tackle puzzles and games but also mentally fitter, sharper, and better prepared for life.

CHAPTER 1
A QUICK GUIDE TO THE BRAIN

Before you embark on a program of exercise, it makes sense to find out a bit about what you are exercising. This chapter provides a quick introduction to the brain, the most important organ in your body, the seat of consciousness, the "wetware," or biological hardware, on which the software of thinking and feeling runs, and the bit you use to tackle your daily Sudoku puzzle.

What is the brain for?

The brain is an organ of control. It controls the systems and processes of the body, while also controlling actions and responses, and, through these, the environment around you. To achieve these varying levels of control, the brain uses several processes. Cells and specialized regions of the brain release chemicals, such as neuro-transmitters and hormones, that affect other brain cells and other parts of the body via the circulatory system. The brain also uses nerve signals—impulses of electrical energy generated and trans-mitted by nerve cells—to communicate with other parts of the body via the nervous system, that connects the brain with the rest of the body via the spinal cord. Perhaps the most important function of the brain is the creation of mental processes that range from the highest level of conscious thought, such as mathematical reasoning or musical creativity, to the lowest level of unconscious regulation, such as triggering the onset of sleep or regulating the level of oxygen in your blood.

Overview of the brain

The brain is essentially the highly developed upper end of the spinal cord. Where the spinal cord enters the base of the skull it swells into the brainstem, that governs unconscious processes such as falling asleep or maintaining blood pressure, and the cerebel-lum, that helps to coordinate body movements. Above and surrounding these is the cerebrum, where emotions, memory, and consciousness are created.

Inside the brain

Between the brainstem and the cerebrum are the limbic system, the thalamus, and the hypothalamus. These structures provide a link between the unconscious processes performed by the brain-stem and the conscious activities of the cerebrum. They are involved in the more "primitive" aspects of being human: emotions, fear, and basic survival drives. They also play essential roles in more "sophisticated" mental abilities, such as learning and memory.

The thalamus and hypothalamus

Information from your senses floods into the thalamus, that sits on top of the brainstem filtering important and relevant information to the cerebrum. It helps to turn conscious decisions into reality. The hypothalamus is a very small area of tissue with a large area of responsibility. As well as helping to control automatic body processes, such as digestion and urine production, it generates basic drives such as hunger, thirst, and even sexual desire.

The limbic system

Most of the brain can be divided into structural groups. The limbic system, however, is a functional group, that includes various structures from different areas of the brain that are involved in functions such as emotion, memory, and learning. Different combinations of the structures perform slightly different functions. For instance, imagine you are walking home one night and encounter a fierce dog. Your amygdala, an almond-shaped structure next to your hypothalamus, helps to produce feelings of fear and apprehension. It also works in conjunction with your hippocampus to link the memory of your canine encounter with the emotions you felt at the time. Your hippocampus works with the mamillary bodies—structures in the base of the hypothalamus—to store these memories, and it is also involved when you are learning a new route home that avoids the dog.

The higher brain

It is in the cerebrum, and in particular on its surface, the cerebral cortex, that the abilities that make us human originate. This is where thought, language, logic, and imagination happen.

The cerebral hemispheres

The outside surface of the brain, the cerebrum, has two obvious features. First, it is extremely wrinkled, which allows a lot of brain to be packed into a small space and maximizes the surface area, or cerebral cortex, where the most active parts are found. Second, it is split lengthwise down the middle to give two halves or hemispheres. Although they look almost identical, the two hemispheres have different functions. They play profoundly different roles in a number of areas—emotion, language, maths—and in the way they deal with information from the senses. Each hemisphere is made up of four lobes, each of which has specialized functions. At the back of the brain are the occipital lobes, that are mainly concerned with vision. At the back and top of the brain are the parietal lobes, that are where sensations from different parts of the body, such as touch and heat, are consciously felt. At the front of the brain are the frontal lobes, where voluntary muscle movements originate and where "higher" intellectual functions, such as planning or mathematical reasoning, are located. At the sides of the brain are the temporal lobes, that are involved in smell, hearing, and language.

Distributed function

Bear in mind that all these descriptions of what happens where in the brain are only intended as rough guides. Mapping brain function is notoriously difficult, and it used to be entirely dependent on postmortem exams of human brains that had a dysfunction, usually as the result of brain damage. One famous case, for instance, was that of Phineas Gage. In 1848, an industrial accident blew a long metal rod through the front of his brain. To everyone's amazement, he recovered physically, but his personality changed overnight. He went from being considerate and responsible to being foul-mouthed, bad-tempered and incapable of making any long-term plans. In 1994, a computer reconstruction showed that Gage had suffered damage to precisely the area now believed to control rational behavior and forethought.

In recent decades, however, more and more advanced scanning techniques have allowed scientists to look at brain activity in real time and to observe what happens where as people perform various types of task. Such scans reveal that while the areas described above may be among the primary hotspots of activity, most of the brain is active at some level and there may be particular hotspots in regions not traditionally associated with the task in hand. In other words, cognitive functions are distributed across the brain.

How the parts of the brain work together

Space precludes a detailed explanation, but here is a whistle-stop tour of how the different parts of the brain act together to produce the amazing range of functions of which it is capable.

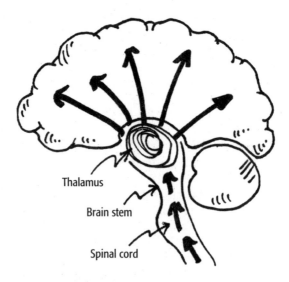

Thalamus

Brain stem

Spinal cord

- Information from your senses, in the form of nerve signals, arrives via the brainstem and passes through the thalami, where signals from differing senses are integrated and the information is routed to other parts of the brain.

A: Association
B: Body sensations
H: Hearing
L: Language
M: Movement
S: Speech
T: Taste
V: Vision

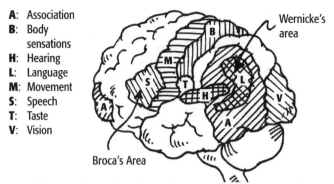

Wernicke's area

Broca's Area

- Sights, sounds, and touch sensations travel to various, specialized portions of the cerebral cortex, where they are processed and analyzed to produce conscious sensations.

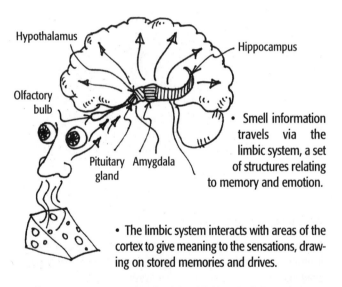

Hypothalamus

Hippocampus

Olfactory bulb

Pituitary gland   Amygdala

- Smell information travels via the limbic system, a set of structures relating to memory and emotion.

- The limbic system interacts with areas of the cortex to give meaning to the sensations, drawing on stored memories and drives.

- The same parts are involved in thinking and formulating a response. Actions, such as speaking or moving, originate as activity in specialized areas of the cortex, and are then implemented with the help of processing by the cerebellum.

CHAPTER 2
MENTAL SPEED

This chapter is about the speed at which your brain processes information and carries out tasks, how you can test that speed and, through practice, how to ensure that you are fulfilling your maximum potential. Sheer mental speed may not seem like the most glamorous or interesting of your mental abilities, but it is possibly the most important one. To understand why, it is necessary to explain how psychologists have investigated intelligence, and how they have arrived at the conclusion that mental speed may be the ultimate basis of intelligence.

Exploring intelligence

This book covers a wide range of tests of mental function; even so, it only scratches the surface of what is available in the world of academia and professional intelligence testing. There are tests for every aspect, component, and subcategory of intelligence that psychologists have thought up, from general knowledge and vocabulary to mental navigation and math. Does this mean that there is no such thing as intelligence, as a single, unitary concept? Do the varied aspects/subcategories of intelligence have anything in common? Is there some sort of underlying factor that ties them together? These are some of the big questions in the field of psychometrics (the study of how psychological factors can be measured), and psychologists use complicated statistical calculations to work out the answers.

Uncovering underlying factors

Time for an analogy. Imagine that you gave a group of 100 people various physical tests. You made them run around a track, swim lengths, dig holes, climb hills, do press-ups, and row on a machine, and you measured how they all did. Some people might be better at running than swimming, while others might be better at rowing than climbing but, on average, you would probably expect there to be some relationship between their performances in the different tests. In other words, you wouldn't expect there to be no relationship between average performance on the rowing machine and average performance on the running track.

In order to prove it, however, you would have to subject their scores to statistical analysis. If you did this, you would find that their scores in different disciplines are related, and you would even be able to put a figure on how closely related—this is known as a correlation. You would almost certainly find that there was one underlying factor that strongly correlated with their scores on all the tests. We could guess that the factor would be physical fitness, and you could try to prove it by devising an exercise that specifically tested physical fitness.

Faster = smarter

The situation with intelligence is similar. When psychologists take scores from lots of different tests and subject them to statistical analysis, they find that there is one factor that strongly correlates with performance on all the tests. They call this factor general intelligence, often referred to as g for short. Exactly what is g? This is

17

still the subject of much debate, but the evidence suggests that g is basically to do with mental speed or processing power. What this means is that if your brain works faster then you are likely to be more intelligent all round. So people with high mental speed are generally better with words, numbers, logic, and all the other aspects of intelligence, and this is why it is important to investigate/exercise your mental speed.

Time trials

Exercises of mental speed are fairly straightforward. They generally involve simple tasks, where the emphasis is on how fast you can do them rather than on how clever you have to be to work them out. Two exercises that are common in IQ tests are digit–symbol coding and symbol search.

Digit–symbol coding

In this exercise you are given a list of symbols that correspond to the digits 0–9, and you have to use this list as a reference for encoding as many numbers as possible in a given amount of time. Look at the example below:

Code:

0	1	2	3	4	5	6	7	8	9
^	Σ	=	–	...	+	μ	~	f	r

Test:

3	7	1	8	2	3	5	0	8	6
–	~	Σ	f	=	–	+			

The top table gives the code you need to follow. The bottom one gives the test items. Your task is to fill in the empty spaces with the symbols that correspond to the numbers directly above them. In the actual exercises (see below), there are 50 items and you are allowed just 30 seconds to see how many you can get. In theory, there are more items than you can do in 30 seconds, but aim to get as close to completing the grid as possible.

This task really is as simple as it looks. It's just a test of how quickly you can cycle through the following series of operations:

1. Identify the number.
2. Look at the code list and locate that number.
3. Identify the symbol that corresponds to that number.
4. Write the corresponding symbol in the blank square.

Steps 1–3 involve mental processing. It may be very low-level, basic mental processing, but it is nonetheless a form of mental work. The faster your mind works, the faster you'll be able to perform this task and the more items you will be able to do in the time allotted.

Several different versions of the exercise are given over the next few pages. It is important for the digits and symbols to be differently encoded each time to prevent you from learning the correspondence, which would make the task easier and remove part of the mental processing required (Stage 2).

For each exercise, use a stopwatch and allow yourself 30 seconds. Don't look at the code table until you've started. When 30 seconds is up, record your score in the space provided. Come back to this exercise later and try again, comparing your scores. Bear in mind that many factors can affect performance including the time of day, how much sleep you got the night before, what you last ate and when, how stressed/calm you are feeling, and even how physically fit you are.

MENTAL SPEED

Digit–symbol coding exercise 1

Code:

0	1	2	3	4	5	6	7	8	9
ƒ	−	=	~	…	^	μ	r	Σ	+

Test:

8	2	3	7	7	0	6	4	3	4
⟨	=	~	⟨	√	ƒ	μ	∴	⌒	…
5	2	1	9	3	6	1	0	4	9
∧	=	ƒ	†	~	μ		ƒ	…	†
4	3	3	7	6	1	8	0	2	5
∴	⌒	~	√						
1	4	0	1	9	8	3	6	1	2
6	4	7	1	3	5	9	0	2	2

Number completed in 30 seconds: ____

MENTAL SPEED

Digit–symbol coding exercise 2

Code:

0	1	2	3	4	5	6	7	8	9
−	μ	+	^	r	...	f	~	Σ	=

Test:

7	4	9	9	2	8	4	6	1	5
9	3	0	1	2	8	3	6	2	0
9	5	8	3	9	2	0	5	1	9
6	8	7	9	4	0	3	9	2	6
3	5	2	3	1	3	2	2	6	7

Number completed in 30 seconds: ____

MENTAL SPEED

Digit–symbol coding exercise 3

Code:

0	1	2	3	4	5	6	7	8	9
μ	^	ʃ	+	^	Σ	>	…	−	~

Test:

4	6	2	1	9	0	8	9	5	1
0	4	3	8	3	6	4	7	8	0
2	5	1	6	3	8	9	2	2	7
3	6	9	4	1	3	7	5	9	5
0	6	6	4	7	1	8	5	9	8

Number completed in 30 seconds: ___

Digit–symbol coding exercise 4

Code:

0	1	2	3	4	5	6	7	8	9
>	…	[]	=	–	+	~	^	ƒ	o

Test:

1	7	6	4	0	7	3	0	1	6
3	9	9	4	1	2	3	4	9	5
5	8	4	1	0	2	4	7	8	0
3	4	2	7	6	3	8	0	9	1
4	5	6	5	1	8	3	9	7	2

Number completed in 30 seconds: ___

Symbol search

This exercise works on similar principles to digit–symbol coding. The task is straightforward and requires only basic levels of processing. What counts is how fast you can do it. You are given a list of symbols, and then have to look at a series of pairs of symbols and identify which symbol in each pair is present in the list. This is shown in the example below:

Symbol list:

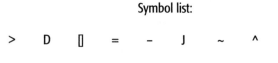

Test pairs:

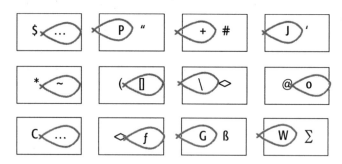

Below are four versions of the exercise. For each one, use a stopwatch and allow yourself 30 seconds. Don't look at the code table until you've started. When 30 seconds are up, record your score in the space provided. Come back to this exercise later and try again, comparing your scores. As with digit–symbol coding, bear in mind that many factors can affect performance.

MENTAL SPEED

Symbol search 1

Symbol list:

>	D	[]	=	⁻	J	~	^	P	o
G	...	+	L	»	\	S	V	}	W

Test pairs:

a P	f \	® ~	á G
o >	\ £	• V	^ ®
... ≠	> ±	D ¥	Σ ...
+ π	ᵃ ~	ƒ }	h o
W ′	» I	J o	á []
® L	D Δ	s =	W ≈
≠ o	À V	≠ D	À ^

Number completed in 30 seconds:____

MENTAL SPEED

Symbol search 2

Symbol list:

£	≠	÷	=	Σ	y	V	D	L	s
»	G	f	W	S	[]	∫	~	}	P

Test pairs:

f　±	S　π	ᵃ　y	[]　Δ
D　©	s　≈	}　À	–　P
f　o	W　J	S　"	Σ　<
>　G	+　÷	$　»	∫　◇
–　~	L　J	÷　@	o　£
+　P	≠　<	}　–	$　s
–　y	\　=	[]　A	Σ　X

Number completed in 30 seconds: ___

MENTAL SPEED

Symbol search 3

Symbol list:

h	G	÷	©	q	Δ	«	\	P	L
$	≠	‡	£	S	fl	@	y	D	s

Test pairs:

‡　C	©　„	fl　•	'　@
–　y	D　»	s　f	J　$
h　C	ß　©	"　÷	Δ　≈
»　«	a　\	D　•	#　÷
G　J	◇　fl	™　h	\　'
y　±	f　≠	$　–	£　a
≈　‡	q　'	≈　Δ	@　'

Number completed in 30 seconds: ___

MENTAL SPEED

Symbol search 4

Symbol list:

[]	~	£	©	=	Δ	«	Σ	p	y
∫	}	‡	^	G	fl	@	\	D	L

Test pairs:

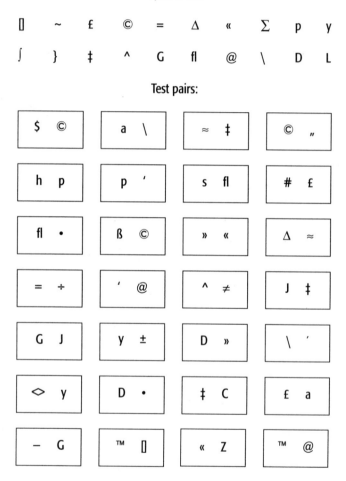

$ ©	a \	≈ ‡	© „
h p	p '	s fl	# £
fl •	ß ©	» «	Δ ≈
= ÷	' @	^ ≠	J ‡
G J	y ±	D »	\ '
◇ y	D •	‡ C	£ a
– G	™ []	« Z	™ @

Number completed in 30 seconds: ___

Speed training

It is thought that mental speed is linked to biological properties of your brain/nerve cells, such as the thickness of the fatty coating that sheathes nerve cells or the rate at which they can pump charged particles in and out. These in turn are determined by the interaction between your genetic blueprint, that was laid down at conception, and the environment you have experienced since then. Crucially, however, these biological properties are probably largely fixed by adulthood, which means that it would be very difficult if not impossible to improve your mental speed through exercise or training.

However, exercise and training *can* help ensure that you exploit your capabilities to the full, so that you reach your maximum potential speed. In particular, they can help to counteract the slowing that accompanies aging.

As well as revisiting the challenges above, you might consider practicing some simple exercises that you can do wherever you go. One in particular that gives you a mental speed "workout" is mental subtraction—a simple form of mental arithmetic where you start with a high number around 100 and repeatedly subtract the same number until you get back to 0. Try subtracting 7 or 9, as these are usually most difficult to do. Although this exercise does involve numerical ability (see Chapter 4) and short-term memory (see Chapter 10), it is also simple enough to be a good test of mental speed. Get into the habit of practicing this exercise during mental "down times" (for example, when going up the escalator, waiting for a bus, hanging out the laundry, etc).

CHAPTER 3
VERBAL
APTITUDE

Many experts think that the evolution of language was the turning point in the evolution of humankind and was responsible for creating the human mind as we know it, as well as for driving many other aspects of human evolution, from the development of large brains to the creation of culture and society. The ability to use words, to manipulate verbal and linguistic concepts, and to master language rules such as grammar and syntax are common attributes of intelligent people, as is a wide vocabulary.

Common sense would suggest that there is a general verbal/language-based type of intelligence that governs performance on different types of verbal/language-based material (such as solving anagrams, spotting synonyms, and completing crosswords), and psychologists have found that this is the case, based on their statistical analysis of people's scores on a range of intelligence tests. For convenience's sake, we can label this type of intelligence "verbal aptitude."

The importance of being verbal

Apart from being a core component of overall intelligence, verbal aptitude is specifically highly relevant to modern careers—everything from marketing and journalism to working in a call center—many of which involve communicating in one way or another through written or verbal media. Even more specifically, verbal aptitude is also one of the main classes of intelligence that are tested in an IQ test, so if you want to achieve your maximum potential IQ score it might pay to swot up on verbal-aptitude skills.

Significantly, for our purposes, verbal aptitude is also a form of intelligence that it may actually be possible to improve through practice. To understand why this is the case, it is necessary to explain the difference between two types of intelligence: fluid and crystallized.

Fluid and crystallized intelligence

Fluid intelligence involves thinking in its most abstract forms—it is about mental agility, adaptability, and speed, and, as such, is closely related to g, the general intelligence factor we looked at in Chapter 2. Abilities closely related to fluid intelligence, or those that are largely "fluid" in nature, include logic and numerical-mathematical questions involving numbers and shapes, such as you'll find in Chapters 4, 5, and 6.

Fluid intelligence can harden or "crystallize" into less abstract, more concrete mental "products," such as knowledge, experience, skills, mental short cuts, and rules of thumb, expertise, etc. One expert has described fluid intelligence as the mechanics of intelligence and crystallized intelligence as the pragmatics. A commonly used analogy is with a machine: the actual machinery is equivalent to fluid intelligence, processing raw materials (equivalent to mental inputs such as sensations, memories, etc) to generate products, that are equivalent to crystallized intelligence.

Language as crystallized intelligence

Among the mental products that constitute crystallized intelligence are vocabulary, grammar, and syntax. In fact, the acquisition of language itself is a prime example of how fluid intelligence becomes crystallized intelligence. A child, who neither speaks nor understands language to begin with, is able to operate on incoming information (the interaction and communication that takes place with parents and others), using his or her natural fluid intelligence, and this crystallizes into a command of the rules, complexities, and subtleties of language.

This process can continue throughout life. You can learn a new language at any age (although due to changes in the wiring of the brain it becomes much harder after puberty kicks in), and you can constantly expand your command of language, and of vocabulary in particular. What this means is that you can actually improve your verbal aptitude, boost your score on the verbal component of IQ tests, and get better at everything from completing crosswords and playing Scrabble to writing reports or composing love poems.

Boost your word power

There are lots of ways to increase your store of crystallized verbal–linguistic intelligence.

- The simplest and possibly the best is to read more. In particular, reading more challenging material will stretch you and teach you new words, new word relations, and new ways of using language. Try reading classics, poetry, popular science, history, and topics and genres that you might not normally consider.
- Write more. Keeping a journal, writing letters, creating stories—all will exercise your powers of expression and your command of language, as well as making you more confident about your language ability (which can help you to relax and focus when tackling verbal-aptitude tasks).

- Learn a language. A new language makes you think more about the formal rules that govern your own and makes you more aware of how your own language is constructed. You may also learn new vocabulary or ways to deduce word meanings by learning about word roots and etymologies. In general, learning a language exercises the brain, forging new connections between nerve cells and, quite possibly, keeping your cortex healthy.
- Word play. Puzzles and games based on letters, words, and language help to maintain your verbal aptitude in peak condition.

Mind at work

Exactly what is going on in your brain when you tackle teasers such as the ones below? The details remain mysterious, but brain scans and studies of people with brain damage and cognitive impairments have revealed, in broad terms, which parts of the brain are active when you think about verbal–linguistic material.

Language foci

Activity is found right across the brain, but there are some particular foci of activity that correspond to areas of the frontal and temporal lobes involved in hearing, formulating words, and speaking them. Of particular importance are two brain regions named after the scientists who first linked them to language roles: Wernicke's area, in the temporal lobe at its junction with the parietal lobe, and Broca's area, at the junction between the frontal and temporal lobes. Wernicke's area is active when you are listening to and making sense of spoken language, while Broca's area is active when you are formulating and producing speech. This suggests that different mental processes are involved in understanding language than are involved in formulating it.

Other areas

In addition to Wernicke's and Broca's areas, however, many other parts of the cortex and the deeper brain are active when you think verbally. This is not surprising, given the range of mental activities involved in language including memory, emotion, perception of time (rhythm, for instance), planning, and muscular coordination. So when you tackle a word puzzle or engage in a conversation with someone, the parts of your brain that are active include the hippocampus and limbic system (that are involved in memory and emotion), the pre-frontal lobes (that are involved in planning), and the motor strip and cerebellum (that are involved in coordination).

Puzzles and challenges

Presented here are a number of puzzles, challenges, and exercises involving words, letters, and language. Some of them are similar to questions you might encounter in an IQ test, others like puzzles you might see in the newspaper. Because they're presented for entertainment/exercise purposes only, it's not necessary to time yourself as you would if they were part of a test.

Anagrams

Anagrams are simple in conception but hard in practice. Solving them depends partly on your knowledge of vocabulary—but this is probably a relatively minor factor (most of the solutions involve common words). More important is your ability to think creatively about letter arrangements, to frame new arrangements in your mind's eye, and to be flexible about this.

Part of what makes an anagram hard is that it is often deliberately presented in a form that makes some sort of sense—for example, another word/phrase, such as the word "leaper" (that is an anagram of "repeal"). Once you have seen "leaper," it can be hard to overcome that conception of the correct arrangement of letters. This is because of the way the mind sometimes works when dealing with stimuli that hang together to form larger units of meaning, as when letters combine to form a word. Once you become expert/fluent in a language, you no longer perceive individual letters, that you then put together to make sounds and syllables, that in turn are processed into words. Instead, you perceive what is known as a "gestalt," from the German for "shape," meaning that you perceive something as a coherent whole rather than as the sum of its parts. Once you have taken in the gestalt "leaper," for instance, it can be hard to shake that word out of its central spot in your mind's eye because the mind is naturally geared up to latch onto gestalts. (As an evolutionary adaptation, it makes good sense for the mind to be a powerful pattern-recognition mechanism and gestalts are a part of this.)

So perhaps the biggest step in solving an anagram is to overcome the initial gestalt and to visualize new arrangements of the letters. It may help to give the rearrangement a concrete form by writing it down, thus overcoming the natural "default" tendency of your mind's eye to revert to the initial gestalt. Another tip is to look for potential word-ending sequences amongst the letters (for example, "-ing" or "-tion"), although these can also be misleading, since you may overlook less obvious endings such as "-le" or "-ab."

Of which words are the following anagrams?

1. SCALAR

2. ACT AS IN

3. BLUE ROT

4. NICE GAL

5. ABLE COP

6. PEE SLOSH

7. BLUEGILL

8. HANG CITY

9. IS OUR LOG

10. REST UNTIL

11. LET ALAN FIB

12. TIBIA TONIC

Bridge word

This is a classic word game where you have to find the word that can complete or combine with both of the given words. For example, if the question was:

1. peace _____ line
the answer would be "pipe," to make "peace pipe" and "pipe line."

Although it seems very different to anagram solving, this exercise involves some similar mental challenges. As with anagrams, it may seem to be a test of vocabulary, but most of the words involved are actually quite common. More importantly, you need to be able to think creatively and to overcome the gestalt presented by having a complete, stand-alone word given to you.

For instance, look at the first item on Challenge 1. Both "book" and "life" are words in their own right, and it can be hard to think past that to see them as part of a phrase or compound word. Equally, there is a tendency to come up with an answer for half of the puzzle, that you are then unable to clear from your mind when it proves to be wrong for the other half. (For example, if you came up with the word "worm" to make "bookworm," you might struggle to clear this solution from your mind.)

Bridge word challenge 1

For each pair of words, find the word that can come after the word on the left and before the word on the right to make two new words or well-known phrases.

1. book _____ life
2. false _____ fairy
3. garden _____ fund
4. green _____ sitter
5. down _____ out
6. ill _____ worker
7. fail _____ cracker
8. smoke _____ bell
9. fire _____ pilot
10. shape _____ work
11. forward _____ hare
12. half _____ lessons
13. full _____ assault
14. tea _____ blower
15. close _____ room
16. water _____ up
17. brown _____ cube
18. tea _____ travel
19. rubber _____ wagon
20. train _____ baron

Bridge word challenge 2

For each pair of words, find the word that can come after the word on the left and before the word on the right to make two new words or well-known phrases.

1. goods _____ wreck
2. high _____ dealer
3. first _____ time
4. bowling _____ room
5. post _____ girl
6. white _____ wheel

7. guide _____ collar
8. pocket _____ block
9. tall _____ teller
10. ticket _____ out
11. soup _____ fed
12. dry _____ worker
13. first _____ wide
14. salmon _____ about
15. quantum _____ frog
16. lead _____ glass
17. hard _____ shape
18. pad _____ smith
19. full _____ shine
20. shot _____ dog

Fictional links

This is an exercise that combines anagram solving—that has a large fluid-intelligence component—with knowledge of culture, a form of crystallized intelligence.

Each question below has a pair of anagrams that, rearranged, spell out the names of two fictional characters who have something in common. Can you work out who they all are? Here is an example to get you started:

"PERT THY ROAR" (5, 6) and "FAG LAND" (7)
Answer: "Harry Potter" and "Gandalf"

1. "PAPER NET" (5, 3) and "A CATKIN HOOP" (7, 4)
2. "FOUL WEB" (7) and "TURK RANG HI" (4, 6)
3. "HI DOORNOB" (5, 4) and "HORRID DELTOID TINGLE" (6, 3, 6, 4)
4. "SAD JOB MEN" (5, 4) and "SEW APRON SUIT" (6, 6)
5. "ADJOIN INSANE" (7, 5) and "CALF OR RAT" (4, 5)
6. "SIR WILT VETO" (6, 5) and "GO SCORE" (7)
7. "NOSE MORPHISM" (5, 7) and "USE ICKY MEMO" (6, 5)
8. "MORE SHELL SHOCK" (8, 6) and "PRIMAL MESS" (4, 6)

Synonyms

Questions involving synonyms (words with similar meanings) and antonyms (words with opposite meanings) are classic components of IQ tests. Like many verbal-aptitude challenges, they test both fluid and crystallized intelligence, although arguably they emphasize the latter, since the key to success is knowledge of vocabulary – you need both knowledge of the words involved and a thesaurus-like ability to come up with similar/opposing ones.

Bear in mind that many of the questions are deliberately tricky or slightly misleading and that the most obvious association may not always be the correct one. You need to think carefully about all the possible meanings of a word and whether just because two words are related or seem to deal with the same topic they are actually synonymous (for instance, the words 'marine' and 'naval' are obviously related in some senses, but they are not synonymous). Also, the question may have two pairs of words that could arguably be the correct answer – in these cases you need to think carefully about which two are the nearest to synonymous.

For each question, circle the two words that are closest in meaning. Here is an example to get you started:

lore   yarn   dogma   superstition   lie

1. design   imagine   discuss   intent   motivate

2. rich   fortune   fate   chance   plan

3 .stern   handle   repulse   gentle   tractable

4. antipathy   mingle   gregarious   friendly   associate

5. vituperative   guileless   scheming   genuine   disinterested

6. lament   praise   paean   eulogy   sing

7. cadence   rhythm   descant   tune   composed

8. disabuse   disturb   displace   distinguish   disburse

9. vainglorious   calm   enervate   innervate   invigorate

10. last   mould   first   finish   pass

Antonyms

Although in a slightly different format, this is essentially the same as 'Synonyms' above, but in this instance you need to work out which words are most opposite in meaning. For example:

Which of these words is most opposite in meaning to 'muted'?

muffled   stunted   gilded   obscure

1. Which of these words is most opposite in meaning to 'vaulting'?

lethargic   overweening   crass   earnest

2. Which of these words is most opposite in meaning to 'amoral'?

lascivious   worthy   pious   disinterested

3. Which of these words is most opposite in meaning to 'sweltering'?

mild   fervid   placid   gelid

4. Which of these words is most opposite in meaning to 'demure'?

diffident   transparent   stark   blatant

5. Which of these words is most opposite in meaning to "churlish"?

truculent   civil   congruent   intelligible

6. Which of these words is most opposite in meaning to "effervesce"?

smolder   gurgle   soothe   deliquesce

7. Which of these words is most opposite in meaning to "hoary"?

contemporary   venerable   penetrable   inspiring

8. Which of these words is most opposite in meaning to "independent"?

autonomous   constrained   cautious   scrupulous

9. Which of these words is most opposite in meaning to "naked"?

manifest   partial   complicated   concealed

10. Which of these words is most opposite in meaning to "clipped"?

terse   short   curt   prolix

Language logic

Although ostensibly similar to the "Synonym" exercise, this game works on different principles. The aim is to figure out the relationship between the two "start" words and then apply the same reasoning to the "test" word and its potential pair. As the name of the game implies, it is a test of logical-reasoning ability. Because the nature of the relationship between the "start" words changes each time, the game also tests your ability to adapt to new patterns of reasoning—to change your way of thinking with each question. This is a key component of fluid intelligence and is something older people often struggle with. Practising tests such as these may, therefore, help to keep your brain youthful and to counteract 'intellectual ageing'.

Remember to read the questions carefully and to ensure that you've understood the governing principle behind each question before picking your answer. Here is an example to get you started:

'Plant' is to 'pot' as 'bulb' is to

flower
lamp
glass
soil

(Just as you find a plant in a pot, so you find a bulb in a lamp.)

1. 'Computer' is to 'programme' as 'brain' is to?

mind
emotion
neuron
head

2. 'Skeleton' is to 'shell' as 'stone' is to?

pip
rind
water
stem

3. 'Starlet' is to 'icon' as 'launch' is to?

rocket
fling
throw
cruiser

4. "Diary" is to "appointment" as "score" is to?

note
goal
mark
strike

5. "Cumulonimbus" is to "rain" as "reservoir" is to?

supply
storage
oil
coal

6. "Torso" is to "limb" as "chassis" is to?

wheel
arch
engine
car

7. "Blunt" is to "whetstone" as "ignorance" is to?

lecture
exam
stupid
teacher

8. "Comedy" is to "drama" as "mammal" is to?

vertebrate
life
whale
reptile

9. "Headline" is to "story" as "abstract" is to?

concrete
paper
idea
art

10. "Point" is to "type" as "stadium" is to?

match
stadia
distance
height

Grid search

This is a good test of your verbal creativity as well as your vocabulary and your ability to mentally assort letters, to assemble and reassemble them into words, and to spot patterns that might give you a clue as to the hidden nine-letter word. Again, this is an exercise where a pen and paper can help by allowing you to set down in black and white arrangements of letters that are different to the ones that may "clog up" your mind's eye—in other words, to overcome the natural tendency to fixate on a word or words you've already discovered, to the extent that it prevents you from spotting others.

Make as many words of four letters or more as you can, using the letters in the grid. All the words must contain the central letter, but you can only use each letter once in each word. Look out for the nine-letter word (these are given in the answers section on page 159). Remember that an "S" can help you to up your score by making plurals, while "D" and "R" can make participles/infinitives of verbs.

1.

E	T	S
R	**A**	A
E	P	D

Target: 36+ = very good; 30–5 = good; under 30 = average

2.

O	P	L
C	**A**	D
E	S	L

Target: 22+ = very good; 18–22 = good; under 18 = average

3.

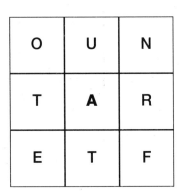

R	P	I
P	**E**	A
N	R	G

Target: 19+ = very good; 15–18 = good; under 15 = average

4.

O	U	N
T	**A**	R
E	T	F

Target: 15+ = very good; 12–14 = good; under 12 = average

Scrambled synonyms
As with "Language logic," this exercise requires you to adapt to new rules with each question, as each question is in a different format. Such adaptability is a key component of fluid intelligence. The fact that each pair of words is made up of two synonyms should help to narrow down the possible range of answers.

The answer to each of the puzzles below is a pair of synonyms. Can you unscramble the letters and fill in the blanks where necessary to discover the words?

1.

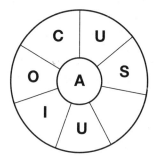 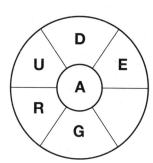

2. To find the word, start in one of the corners and cycle round in either direction, finishing with the central letter and filling in the blanks.

	U	B
I	L	E
T	U	

	I		S
N	G	I
R	A	

3. "COVET TRIPE" and "EVE SIPS SOS"

4. "ADD TIDAL PIE" and "SHIELD DELVE"

Author, Author!

Guess the name of the famous writer using the clues, that are synonyms for the syllables of the writer's surname. They start off difficult and get harder. Like "Fictional links," this is partly a test of crystallized intelligence in the form of knowledge of literature, but it is primarily a test of your ability to think creatively and laterally when it comes to words, word meanings, sounds, and synonyms. Here is an example to get you started:

disease   over
Answer: Blyton (disease = blight; over = on)

1. grinder	weight	
2. cleverness	male	
3. agitate	assegai	
4. lexicon	value	
5. tariff	eager	
6. fuel	corrugation	
7. dimension	collapsed	indebted
8. leap	atmosphere	
9. trimming	route	
10. alcove	mistake	

Mysteries of English

See if you can work out the answers to these eight questions. Some require knowledge of the wider mysteries of the English language, others can be worked out with a combination of observation and simple logic. Part of the challenge is to figure out which is which. As with "Language logic," you will need to adapt quickly to changing mental demands—to be flexible in the application of reason and the selection of the type of information you focus on.

This ability is a key component of fluid intelligence. Much of the content of these questions, however, involves crystallized intelligence (for example, command of vocabulary), making this a good test of fluid and crystallized verbal–linguistic intelligence working in combination.

1. What does the following string of letters represent?
e t a o i n s r h l d c u m f p g w y b v k x j q z

2. What do these five words have in common?
pod   unkindness   parliament   drove   bed

3. What is particular about this list of US states?
Texas   Kansas   Arizona   Illinois   Minnesota
Washington   Mississippi

4. What does the following string of letters represent?
o t t f f s s e n t

5. What do these six words have in common?
flour   feat   threw   loot   mall   climb

6. What does the following string of letters represent?
e t d s

7. What do these six words have in common?
black   pigeon   cake   bolt   fishing   rabbit

8. What do these four words have in common?
moose   sheep   fish   grass

CHAPTER 4
NUMERICAL APTITUDE

Animals can count. This is the surprising discovery of experiments with animals as diverse as dolphins, parrots, and chimpanzees, and it shows that a sense of number–known as numerosity–is not unique to the human species. Undoubtedly unique to us, however, are the higher forms of mathematical ability that stretch far beyond numerosity into the realm of pure math held by great minds throughout history to be the highest attainment of human cognition. Such rarefied realms have little relevance for most of us in our day-to-day lives, but numerical–mathematical aptitude is a central element of everyday intelligence, however wary most people may feel about math.

What is numerical aptitude?

The first thing to point out is that (for our purposes) the terms "numerical aptitude," "mathematical aptitude" and "numerical–mathematical aptitude" are, to some extent, interchangeable. They all refer to the ability to work with numbers. At the most basic level, this means skills as simple as counting, perceiving numbers of objects at a glance (technically known as subitizing), and being able to tell which number is larger and which smaller (known as intuition of number size). The step up from this is simple mental arithmetic, such as addition and subtraction. Multiplication and division are another step up, and beyond these are abilities such as complex mental arithmetic, algebra, the ability to perceive numerical and mathematical patterns, and advanced mathematical concepts such as calculus.

Everyday life rarely involves much more than mental arithmetic, but this is, nonetheless, an important and complex ability. It requires you to perceive and to store numbers, to manipulate them by performing mental operations on them, to store the products of these operations, and then to manipulate them further. Even people who discount their numerical ability and fear math routinely perform these kinds of functions when shopping, checking their bank balance or working out how much a night out is going to cost.

Where in the brain does math happen?

Like most higher mental activities, numerical–mathematical thinking involves many disparate regions of the brain acting in concert. For instance, there is a major element of planning involved in working out a complex sum that might involve the pre-frontal cortex, while plotting a graph or doing geometry requires conception and mental manipulation of space and form (see Chapter 5) that might involve regions of the right temporal lobe.

However, research into patients with brain damage that causes specific loss of numerical aptitude, together with brain-scan studies, have fingered a specific region of the brain: the left inferior parietal lobe. This portion of the cortex is active when you perform basic numerical–mathematical thinking such as counting and judging differences between numbers. More complex mathematical thinking probably involves more and different areas of the brain, in particular the frontal lobe.

Are men better at math?

It has been suggested that the mathematical parts of the brain might be different in men and women, because there seems to be a discrepancy between male and female achievement in the field of math. This is a controversial subject. When Harvard President Lawrence Summers spoke on the issue in January 2005, his injudicious comments led to a media firestorm, and the university felt compelled to donate 50 million dollars to the promotion of gender equality. So what is the truth? Are men better at math?

Average Joes and Average Josephines
In some ways, the row about gender differences in numerical–mathematical aptitude is bogus, because almost everyone agrees that for 99 percent of the population there is no innate difference in ability. There are few significant differences between average male and female scores on tests of numerical aptitude, and male and female students, up to undergraduate level, do just as well as each other. In some applied fields, such as accountancy, women may eventually outnumber men. Where there are differences, most people agree that they are due to socio-cultural influences, that tend to encourage boys to do math and physics, while directing girls to more "gender-appropriate" subjects such as English and psychology.

The bell curve
What is at issue is what happens at the extreme ends of the mathematical aptitude range. When you measure people for an attribute, whether it be height, weight, memory power, or intelligence, it is

usually the case that their scores will follow a pattern known as a normal distribution, where most of the scores cluster around a central peak (the average score) and then get less common the further you get from this average. Plotted on a graph it looks like this, and is sometimes called a bell curve:

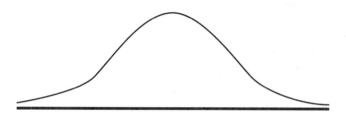

Extremes of intelligence
Towards the far left and right of this curve you find the extremes of human attributes. If this were a graph of heights in the population, people at either extreme would be the unusually tall or the unusually short ones—probably people with genetic or hormonal conditions such as dwarfism or gigantism. If you plotted a graph of people's scores on tests of numerical–mathematical aptitude, you'd get a similar curve. Most people would score close to the average, and there would be a few exceptionally good or exceptionally bad performers at either extreme. The far right of the graph would represent mathematically gifted people, prodigies, and geniuses.

The argument about gender differences focuses on this extreme end of the spectrum of mathematical ability, because the evidence suggests that men significantly outnumber women in this region. In other words, there are far more male mathematical prodigies and geniuses than female ones, and this gender difference may apply to the entire field of math above an undergraduate level, where very complex, abstract, "pure" mathematical thinking is required.

A good head for figures?
The figures are fairly unequivocal about this gender gap—it does

exist. The real question is why. Some scientists think it is down to actual physical differences between male and female brains: the "mathematical" portions of the brain do not grow as large or develop as much in women as they do in men. This is controversial, and many other scientists argue that it is more down to socio-cultural influences, the same ones that discourage school-girls from studying engineering.

Ultimately, this debate is literally academic in nature, because the gender difference mainly affects academics. It is worth remembering that for the vast majority of the population, individual differences in numerical aptitude are far greater than average gender differences.

Math-anxiety

Something that affects both genders, but particularly women, is math-anxiety: irrational fear of mathematical challenges/tasks and a conviction that one cannot cope with math. This can manifest itself in many forms, from a tendency to throw one's hands up in defeat when faced with a mathematical brainteaser to a refusal to balance checkbooks or work out domestic budgets.

The roots of math-anxiety

Math-anxiety may have multiple causes. In some countries, mathematical ability is perceived as a socially undesirable trait—in other words, math is for nerds. Anti-math bias may particularly affect girls and women, with socio-cultural pressures from early school years onward tending to reinforce the message that math is not for girls. Poor teaching of math can lead to negative early experiences, priming math-anxiety from an early age and leading to a series of self-fulfilling prophecies. For instance, if you shy away from math because you think you can't do it and, as a result, don't learn how to do it properly, you will indeed struggle to pass exams. Math-anxiety becomes a "learned response."

A number of math myths tend to back up learned math-anxiety, such as the belief that math is strictly for accountants, actuaries, and other "soulless automatons," or that it can only be done by people with "math brains"–people who have a special numerical–mathematical aptitude. As this chapter should demonstrate, while people may vary along a spectrum of numerical aptitude, everyone has some degree of ability. Mathematical ability is built into all human brains, which makes sense given the fundamental nature of math. The 19th-century Irish mathematician Henry J. S. Smith wrote: "Poor teaching leads to the inevitable idea that [math] is only adapted to peculiar minds, when it is the one universal science, and the one whose ground rules are taught us almost in infancy and reappear in the motions of the universe."

Overcoming math-anxiety

Math-anxiety is similar to many other forms of anxiety/phobia. Overcoming it requires patience, commitment, and the will to learn coping strategies. The first step is to acknowledge its existence, to recognize where and how it affects you, and to identify how it could be damaging your day-to-day life and your career prospects. Then you need to articulate and challenge the counterproductive assumptions that underlie your anxiety and gain the confidence to overcome them. Take small steps–gradually you can build up to tackling more difficult math problems until you can cope with anything you meet in everyday life.

The benefits of boosting your numerical aptitude

It is easy to dismiss math as an esoteric pursuit with little relevance to daily life. In practice, numerical aptitude is called upon for a surprising range of everyday activities as well as more specialized ones. According to one estimate, fewer that 25 percent of careers involve no math, and these tend to be the less skilled, lower-paying ones. So boosting your numerical aptitude could make you money. It could also save you money. Many people pay unnecessary charges, fees, and interest because they don't balance their books properly or budget intelligently.

Numerical aptitude is a mainly fluid form of intelligence (although crystallized intelligence does play a part in terms of learned approaches to problem-solving and in recognizing mathematical constructs and patterns). As such, it is closely bound up with your core, general intelligence and anything you can do to exercise it may help to exercise your general intelligence as well. As we saw in the Introduction, a program of mental exercise can form a core element of braintenance. Exercising your numerical aptitude could be one of the most effective forms of mental workout.

Math puzzles and challenges

Below is a range of puzzles, challenges, and exercises—from the fairly basic to the more involved—to test your numerical aptitude. Unless it is specifically mentioned, you should not use a calculator, although you might find it helps to use a pen and a piece of paper. As a general rule, however, wherever possible do the arithmetic in your head. Mental arithmetic itself is a good mental exercise, drawing on your short-term memory powers as well as your numerical aptitude and, thus, gives each test an extra element of mental workout.

Fractions to percentages
This is a fairly straightforward exercise where you have to recast fractions in percentage form (for example, ½ = 50%). It is a useful way of getting you to think about the relations between numbers and to do some simple mental arithmetic, but it is also good training for other, more complex exercises, because you will meet fractions and percentages in many other questions/guises. Many of the questions below might look daunting, but you should remember that they have been specifically selected so that they do not require you to use a calculator, do any long division or deal with fiddly decimals. Look more closely at each question and you will see that there is a relatively simple relationship between the numbers, especially in terms of working out percentages.

1. $^{25}/_{125}$ = _____

2. $^{120}/_{40}$ = _____

3. $^{66}/_{99}$ = _____

4. $^{84}/_{112}$ = _____

5. $^{45}/_{75}$ = _____

6. $^{8}/_{5}$ = _____

7. $^{225}/_{50}$ = _____

8. $^{99}/_{132}$ = _____

9. $^{24}/_{40}$ = _____

10. $^{21}/_{20}$ = _____

Logical progression

This is a very different kind of exercise. It involves a major element of logical thinking and is, thus, a strong test of fluid intelligence. Your task is to identify the pattern or guiding principle behind each series of numbers and then to apply that logic to deduce the next in the series. For instance, if the series was: "2, 4, 6, 8, 10," you might surmise that the guiding principle was to increase in increments of 2, so that the next in the series would be 12. The actual questions are tougher than this and generally get harder as you work down the list. Remember that the relationship between the numbers won't always involve arithmetic or some other obvious mathematical property. You need to be adaptable and creative in your thinking. For each sequence of numbers, work out the missing number:

1. 3, 9, 27, 81, _____

2. 100, 50, 33.33, 25, 20, 16.66, 14.29, _____

3. 1, 10, 11, 100, 101, 110, _____

4. 1, 1, 2, 3, 5, 8, _____

5. 4, 9, 16, 25, 36, _____

6. 1, 3, 5, 7, 11, _____

7. 987, 610, 377, 233, 144, _____

8. 1, 2, 6, 24, 120, 720, _____

9. 1, 9, 25, 49, 121

10. 33, 31, 34, 30, 35, 29, _____

11. $\frac{3}{6}$, $\frac{4}{12}$, $\frac{5}{20}$, _____

12. 13, 26, 39, 52, 5, 18, 31, 44, 57, _____

13. 90, 56, 30, _____

14. 81, 18, 64, 16, 49, 14, _____ and _____

15. 12, 15.5, 19.5, 24, 29, _____

16. 2, 4.5, 8, 12.5, 18, _____

17. 0, 1000, 50, 950, 150, 850, 350, 650, 750, _____

18. 11, 13, 17, 25, 32, _____

19. 5, 7.2, 10.5, 14.9, 20.4, _____

20. 123, 466, 161812, 645424, _____

Math grid

Fill in the grids based on the numerical reasoning evident from the occupied spaces. For example:

3	12	21
6	15	24
9	18	27

The two empty squares would be 21 and 27, on the basis that the grid is filled by the three times table running in columns. In the actual test, the grid may be filled in by row, in a spiral, or in any other configuration. There may be a progression from one square to the next, or the rules governing the cube may not involve any form of progression but follow some other logic.

NUMERICAL APTITUDE

Challenge 1

13		
8	1	1
5	3	2

Challenge 2

1	2	
4	4	8
5	6	

Challenge 3

2	4	6
3	6	9

Challenge 4

4	7	2
9	6	5
1		8

Challenge 5

34	41	46
104		56
88	80	67

Challenge 6

8	7	12
5		5
3	1	

Challenge 7

32	30	26
27	21	13
65	55	

Challenge 8

2	5	8
7	6	9
12	11	

Challenge 9

	5	
7	11	77
	17	221

Challenge 10

001	101	1001
010	110	1010
100	1000	

Odd one out

This is a similar challenge to "Logical progression" in that you have to work out what the guiding pattern/logic is behind the group of numbers and then use this information to figure out which one does not belong. For instance, in the sequence, "12, 8, 2, 16, 5, 10, 22," 5 is the odd one out because all the others are even numbers. The actual questions are harder than this, and as with "Logical progression," you need to think creatively and adapt your thought processes to a new challenge with each question. You may want to use a calculator for some of these questions, although for most of them it isn't necessary.

1. 0.37 + 0.13, $\frac{1}{3}$ of 1.5, 10 x 0.2, $\frac{2}{3}$ x $\frac{3}{4}$
Odd one out: _____

2. 479, 145, 786, 278, 167, 468
Odd one out: _____

3. $\frac{4}{16}$ x $\frac{81}{27}$, $\frac{118}{472}$ x $\frac{24}{8}$, $\frac{36}{12}$ x $\frac{18}{72}$, $\frac{21}{7}$ x $\frac{9}{27}$
Odd one out: _____

4. $\frac{160}{125}$, $\frac{40}{32}$, $\frac{46}{36}$, $\frac{28}{16}$
Odd one out: _____

5. 132 + 99, 254 + 190.5, 96 + 74, 88 + 66, 116 + 87
Odd one out: _____

6. 33.33, 20, 14.29, 9.09, 8.33, 7.69
Odd one out: _____

7. $^{55}/_{11}$, $^{323}/_{17}$, $^{108}/_{18}$, $^{168}/_{56}$, $^{134}/_{28}$
Odd one out: _____

8. 117, 243, 180, 422, 351
Odd one out: _____

9. 63, 34, 49, 19, 76, 22
Odd one out: _____

10. 842, 641, 613, 907, 411, 530
Odd one out: _____

Practical math

You may argue with the description "practical," but these sorts of questions at least hint at how numerical aptitude can help solve real-life problems. These are also the sorts of questions that math-phobics may have most trouble with, because it is often not at all obvious how to go about solving them, and the temptation is to write them off as impossible. To solve them you need to think logically, to consider whether the question gives you more information than you realize (for instance, if you are supplied with an average and the number of examples, you can work out a total), and, if necessary, to try out some possible solutions by plugging guesstimates into your calculations to see if they give the right answer. You will probably find it helpful to use a pen and paper for some of these questions, but none of them requires a calculator.

1. Four years from now my grandmother will be twice the combined ages of my two children. Three years ago the aver-

age age of my children was sixteen. How old is my grand-mother now?

2. Rory the Jack Russell lives in a square pen, that is 5 yards along each side. He loves to bury bones, but he's a very precise dog. Each bone burial takes up an area of exactly 1yard squared, and Rory hates to overlap his burial plots. Mungo the St Bernard lives in the pen next door to Rory. The pen is also square, but its sides are twice as long. Mungo buries his bones in the same fashion as Rory but, being bigger, he takes up 2 yards squared with each bone. Which dog can fit the most bones in their pen?

3. Rufus weighs three times as much Max, but if they both gain 56 pounds, Max will weigh half as much as Rufus. How much do they each weigh now?

4. Dominic the flower-seller sells eight carnations for every five roses. At the end of the day he's sold 160 carnations. How many roses did he sell?

5. Ernie the postman has to finish his round at midday, but he's still got three letters to deliver. The first one has to go to Prime Number Gardens, which is $1\frac{1}{2}$ miles away from where he is now. The next one has to go to Factorial Villas, which is $\frac{3}{4}$ mile past Prime Number Gardens. The last letter has to go to Pi Mansion, which is 3 miles further than Factorial Villas. From Pi Mansions back to the sorting office, it's $2\frac{1}{4}$ miles. Ernie has a bicycle, and his average speed (when the time it takes to get off the bike and post the letters is included) is 15 miles per hour. What's the latest he can set off and still make it back to the sorting office by midday?

6. In 2004, Stan the stockbroker bought $1 million worth of shares, which lost 40 percent of their value by the end of the year. In 2005, however, the share value went up by 60 per-cent of its value at the start of the year. Ivan the investor put his $1 million in the bank at a compound interest rate of 5 percent per annum. Whose investment was worth more at the start of 2006?

7. The SuperEuro train, non-stop from London to Paris, travels at 180 kilometers per hour. It takes 4 seconds to pass a man standing on the platform at Ashurst where it enters the Channel Tunnel, and it then takes exactly 15 minutes and 28 seconds for the entire length of the train to pass through the tunnel and come out the other side. Exactly how long, in meters, is the Channel Tunnel?

8. Freddy the forester had to cut down three trees with a combined height of 728 feet. The first tree was 54 feet higher than the second one and 73 feet higher than the third one. How tall was each tree?

9. Traveler Tim is trying to figure out the basketball scores from a scrap of newspaper he's come across which gives the results from two games. He knows that the average combined score was 212, that the Falcons beat the Warthogs by 10 points, and in doing so scored 3 points more than the Wolverines who tied their game with the Pirates. What were the scores?

10. Paula, Pippa, and Pam are playing poker. In Poker, seeing someone means meeting their bet with an equal bet, raising them means equalling it and then increasing it. For everyone to have "seen" everyone else, they all need to have bet the same amount last, although it may take several round of betting for this to happen. Paula bets a quarter of her chips, Pippa raises her $5, and Pam sees that and raises her another $10. Paula and Pippa both see her, and Pam wins the pot, raking in a cool $90. How many dollars' worth of chips did Paula have at the start of the hand?

Box o' numbers

In some ways, this challenge is like an extension of the "Math grid" exercise in that you have to work out the rules that govern the placement of numbers in each box, except that there is an added element of logic required to figure out what the progression is from one box to the next, as well as within each box. You may find a calculator helpful with one of these questions.

NUMERICAL APTITUDE

Challenge 1

2	6	10
6	10	14
10	14	18

4	8	12
8	12	16
12	16	20

6		

Challenge 2

4
8
12

6
12
18

9
18

Challenge 3

2
3
4

4
9
16

8
27

Challenge 4

12
7
5

23
16
7

14
5

Challenge 5

6
1
3

4
2
4

3
2

Challenge 6

16
4
2

25
5

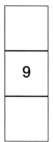

9

Challenge 7

12	9
40	30
32	24

56	28
18	9
8	4

48	12
120	
28	

Challenge 8

7	7
6	8
5	9

11	11
9	13
7	15

24	24

Challenge 9

32	8
4	2
2	1

40	20
2	10
0.2	50

72	12
	$\frac{2}{3}$

Challenge 10

5
10
2

20
3
1$\frac{2}{3}$

5
5

CHAPTER 5
SPATIAL APTITUDE

Most people are familiar with the idea of thinking specifically about words or numbers and are, therefore, comfortable with the concept of verbal or numerical aptitude. Spatial aptitude may be a less familiar concept, but in many ways it is a much more universal aspect of mental life. Spatial aptitude or, to use a broader term, spatial intelligence, is concerned with visual experience and the related world of forms, dimensions, patterns, shapes, movement, navigation and, of course, space. Spatial aptitude is called on when you reach out to grab something, put your shopping away in the kitchen closets, work out how long it will take you to get to the stores, plan the drive to your folks' place or draw a diagram of how you want the living room to look when you get that new sofa in. It is essential to sportspeople, architects, engineers, and artists, but also to housewives, shelf-stackers, and students.

Mental models

One school of thought says spatial intelligence is central to intelligence in general and maybe even to the whole concept of mind. According to this way of thinking, the mind works mainly by constructing mental models of the world, of other people, of time and causality, and so on. These models may be abstractions of a purely conceptual nature, but, the argument goes, they nonetheless exist in a mental space—the elements relate to one another, they have conceptual dimensions, order, and other qualities of space and form. Since spatial intelligence governs this mental space and the models that are formed in it, it could be argued that spatial intelligence underlies or is essential to the operation of mind and intelligence.

Reaction and choice

There is experimental evidence to back up this idea. As we discussed in Chapter 2, the general intelligence factor, g, seems to be related to mental speed. The primary evidence for this is that IQ scores relate to simple tests of mental speed such as reaction time, as tested in experiments where people see how fast they can push a button when it lights up. Faster reaction times seem to be linked to higher IQ scores.

But more detailed investigation of these results suggests that when an element of choice is introduced (for example, if there are several buttons and the subject has to decide which one to react to—a bit like a laboratory version of Hungry Hungry Hippos), the experiment is a better predictor of IQ. In other words, how fast you are able to use your spatial intelligence to complete the task (hitting the right button) may be strongly linked to your IQ, suggesting that spatial intelligence, or something about it, is fundamental to general intelligence. (When we say "a better predictor", what is meant is that a person's score on this test correlates more strongly with his or her IQ than in the other, simpler tests. This suggests that the more sophisticated test involves a higher degree of the mental processes that might be described as "pure intelligence.")

A different kind of mind

Another school of thought holds that spatial intelligence is more than just a facet of general intelligence, closely related to verbal and numerical aptitude. According to this interpretation, spatial intelligence is dramatically different and separate from verbal intelligence and the two may even work antagonistically at times. One piece of evidence for this is what is called the dual coding theory of memory, that says that there are two types of memory operating in parallel: memory for words and memory for images. You can show this experimentally by getting a subject to attempt two memory tasks in rapid succession. If they both involve the same sort of memory (for example, if both involve words or both involve images) you see an effect called interference, where attempting to do the second task interferes with your performance on the first task. If the two tasks involve different types of material (for example, "remember some words, then remember some pictures"), you find that this interference effect is much less pronounced. This suggests that there are indeed two different types of memory system, perhaps reflecting a wider difference in the way the brain handles verbal and spatial information. (For more on memory, see Chapter 10.)

Problem kids

The pictures versus words theory might sound interesting but fairly trivial. However, some psychologists think that this distinction between verbal and spatial could explain a host of issues connected with learning difficulties and disruptive children. According to this theory, both our education system and wider society have focused primarily on verbal intelligence—children are taught mainly verbal information in a mainly verbal way. Many careers and other aspects of adult life also reflect this emphasis, but what this fails to show, says psychologist Thomas G. West, a leading proponent of this view, is that for the vast majority of human evolution, society was pre-literate. Spatial intelligence used to be more important to success and survival than verbal intelligence (or at least, far more vital than it is now).

Even today, many people have a primarily spatial intelligence. For them, West argues, the normal, verbal paradigm of school and education is a bad fit, and they are labeled as deficient or dysfunctional and diagnosed with disorders such as dyslexia, autism, attention deficit disorder, and other behavioral and learning problems. Far from being deficient, however, many of these children may, in fact, be gifted in non-verbal skills that can lead to the sort of inventive, creative thinking that society needs. West points to figures such as Albert Einstein, Michael Faraday, Thomas Edison, Nikola Tesla, and Winston Churchill as examples of spatially intelligent people who were considered unpromising in their youth but who went on to achieve great things. Whether or not theories such as West's are correct, they suggest that spatial aptitude may be an underrated form of intelligence.

Lost on Venus?

An interesting feature of spatial aptitude is that it is one of the few areas where tests routinely show a significant gender difference in performances. In particular, men do better than women (on average) in tasks such as mental rotation (see pages 77–80) and object-tracking (where you have to track a moving object). Psychologists have related this to the finding that men tend to be better at tasks that involve aiming and throwing. All of this suggests several gender stereotypes: "Girls can't throw," "Don't ask a woman to read a map," etc. Is this fair?

There are two points to make here. First, the tasks where a gender difference has been shown are quite specific and, while they may back up the "Girls can't throw" stereotype, they're not specific for map reading or navigation (although further studies may change this). Second, the differences we're talking about are average differences between groups and should not be misapplied to individuals. It is worth quoting at length part of the American Psychological Association's 1995 special taskforce report, "Intelligence, Knowns and Unknowns":

Group means [average scores within a group] have no direct implications for individuals. What matters for the next person you meet (to the extent that test scores matter at all) is that person's own particular score, not the mean of some reference group to which he or she happens to belong. The commitment to evaluate people on their own individual merit is central to a democratic society. It also makes quantitative sense. The distributions of different groups inevitably overlap, with the range of scores within any one group always wider than the [average] differences between any two groups. In the case of intelligence test scores, the variance attributable to individual differences far exceeds the variance related to group membership.

The meaning of the last sentence is that individual factors—such as the genes you inherited from your parents, the environment you experienced in the womb, in childhood and later, the education you received, the food you ate and the pollution to which you were exposed—have a far larger influence on how much your performance differs from the person standing next to you than whether that person is male or female or black or white.

Boost your spatial aptitude

As we've already discussed, spatial aptitude is regularly called on in everyday life, but to maximize your potential and to really give yourself a spatial-intelligence workout, you need to push yourself a bit further than the everyday. Below are a series of tests, teasers, and challenges to get your mind's eye working and to tickle your spatial thought processes.

Most involve some sort of spatial reasoning, but what you won't find in this chapter are the sorts of questions that many people associate with IQ tests and mental workouts the most—where you are given a series of diagrammatic elements (for example, circles with spots and triangles in them) and asked to work out the next in the series. This kind of logical progressive reasoning exercise, sometimes called progressive matrices, is found in Chapter 6 (on logical aptitude) because, although they do involve spatial reasoning, they are primarily tests of logic. The questions/exercises here mostly involve imagery and the ability to create and manipulate mental models/representations of space and form.

Another brick in the wall

This next test is based on a simple expression of visual intelligence and the mind's capacity to form models—in other words, on your ability to look at two-dimensional shapes and to translate them into three-dimensional ones in your mind's eye. To complete this test, you have to visualize what might be going on behind the blocks that you can see, working from the sketchiest of visual cues (there may be little more than a horizontal line). You also need to pay close attention to the instructions.

Assuming that raised blocks must be supported from beneath by other blocks, what is the minimum number of blocks there must be in each of the following constructions?

Challenge 1

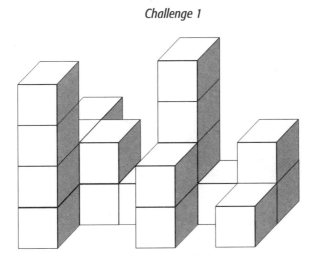

Challenge 2

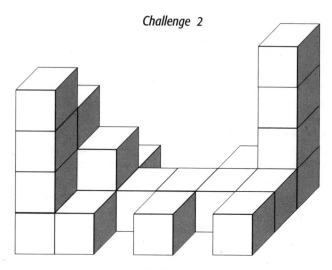

Challenge 3

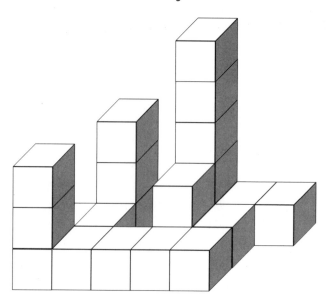

Challenge 4

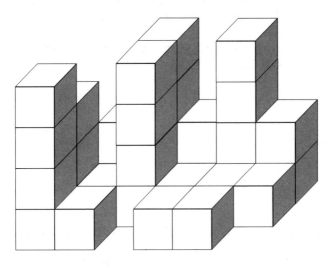

Mental rotation

With objects in the real world, we are accustomed to handling them, turning them to look at them from different angles, or perhaps moving ourselves if the object is too large for this. For a mental object, such as the image that you form when you look at the shapes in the exercise below, such manipulation must be mental in nature, and this can prove to be a tricky task. In this test of your ability to mentally rotate an image, you need numerical–spatial ability (to turn an instruction that uses degrees into a mental operation) and working memory (especially when there is more than one step in the instruction).

This latter part, in particular, can cause problems, because it can be tricky to store a purely mental image (the initial image is the one presented to you in print, that acts as a physical substitute for memory, but after you've completed the first step in the instructions, you need to store the changed image in your working memory so that you can then apply to it the operation described in the second step).

The smart test-taker looks for shortcuts to avoid difficulties like this. Think about the instructions carefully—in IQ-test style questions they are often deliberately designed to be simplifiable.

1. What would the following shape look like if you rotated it 135 degrees clockwise?

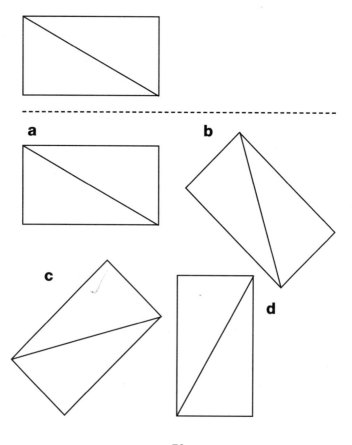

2. What would the following shape look like if you rotated it 180 degrees anticlockwise, and then 90 degrees clockwise?

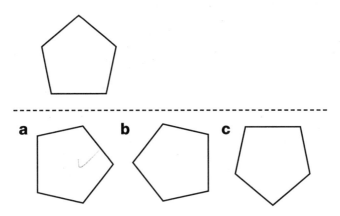

3. What would the following shape look like if you rotated it 450 degrees clockwise?

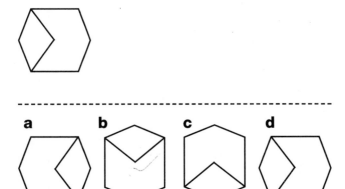

4. What would the following combination of shapes look like if you rotated the crescent 270 degrees clockwise and the circle 45 degrees anticlockwise?

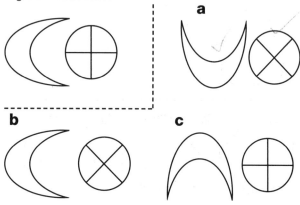

5. What would the following shape look like if you rotated it 90 degrees clockwise and then 270 degrees anticlockwise?

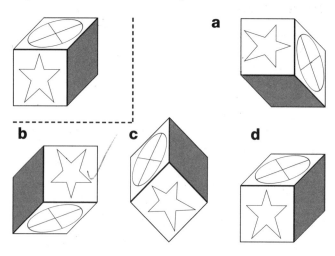

Picture completion

This exercise involves perceptual/observational skills as well as spatial reasoning, although the latter may not be immediately obvious. At first glance this might look like "Where's Wally?" or a similar game for kids, but the point here is that the exercise cannot be completed simply by spotting the missing element. The candidate elements are deliberately simple to the point of being abstract, and in most cases all of them *could* be added to the picture. What you need to work out is which one is *definitely* missing, based on visual logic.

Look at the pictures below. Each one is missing an element. Which of the five options would best fit the picture?

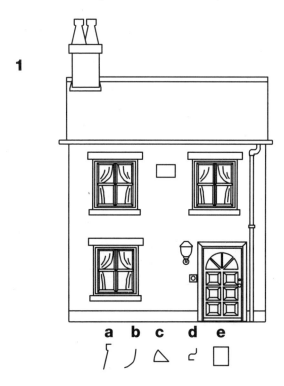

1

a   b   c   d   e

2

a   b   c   d   e

3

a   b   c   d   e

4

a   b   c   d   e

Mental navigation

One aspect of spatial aptitude is the ability to create and explore mental maps—mental representations of the geography and topography of the real world. This may sound esoteric, but it is probably one of the most universal and commonplace mental abilities. Everyone carries in their head mental representations of spaces and places from bedrooms to the layout of their hometown to the face of the planet. Everyone routinely works out distances, routes, estimated times of transit, and spatial relations of one place/thing to another (for example, Chuck's Bar is in the West End, that is north of the train station; or the sofa is on the right of the coffee table, that sits facing the french doors), all of which require the use of mental maps.

One way to hone this facility is to try some mental navigation challenges/exercises. The exercises below also involve, and therefore work out, other mental skills such as visualization and memory.

Map maker

Test your memory as well as your navigational sense with a simple exercise. Starting in the middle of a clean sheet of paper, map out your local area. Try to keep the distances between streets and blocks in the same proportion as in reality. Mark out as many side roads and alleyways as you can visualize/remember. See how far from your house you can get in each direction before your knowledge of local geography runs out.

Remote viewing

A sort of reverse exercise is to get hold of a map and to use it as the basis for visualization. Find a detailed map of an area, such as a streetmap or a survey map. You don't need to be familiar with the area. Pick a spot at random and use the information on the map to visualize the area from different points of view. Begin with a bird's-eye perspective, like that of the map, but then switch to a ground-level perspective, as if you were standing in the spot you picked and are looking around you. Use the symbols and contours shown on the map to visualize the topography of the area, the lie of the land, any landmarks or buildings you can see. If you enjoy drawing, try sketching the view that you would see at each point of the compass.

For a variation on this exercise, draw a straight line on your map from where you are now to a distant target location. Using the information on the map, draw the skyline someone looking directly along that line would see.

Location, location, location

For this exercise, you need a detailed map of your town, city, or local area. Go to an upper-floor window, or up a hill if you can't find a view from indoors. Look out across the city or local area. Pick a spot that you can see, but with which you are not familiar (in other words, not a landmark), and take a good look at it. Now see if you can identify exactly where it is on your map. Orient the map to copy your actual orientation with regard to the spot you have picked. Try to visualize how you would get from where you are now to the target spot.

For a variation on this game, take a map with you on the bus or train and use it track your real-world movement, to work out where you are at any given moment and to predict which roads, intersections, and landmarks will come into view.

Miscellaneous spatial-aptitude test

This test comprises a variety of question formats to test various aspects of spatial aptitude and also to test your adaptability as you switch between these aspects. Prominent among the different aspects is your ability to use your mind's eye to visualize the problems and, literally, to look for the solutions. Exactly what is the "mind's eye"? The popular conception is probably something akin to a mini movie screen in your brain onto which your imagination projects images, that in turn are viewed by whatever part of your consciousness constitutes your central, observing self. In fact, this is not far off the truth, if experiments with brain scans and visualization tasks are to be believed. Scientists have found that when people are asked to visualize an image, the part of the cortex associated with vision becomes active, and it does so in a topographically appropriate way—that is to say that the area activated is related to the size and shape of the image being visualized. Incredibly, modern technology makes it possible to disrupt this mental video screen. If a wand that generates a strong magnetic field is placed near the back of the head, where the mind's eye seems to be located, the activity of the neurons in that area is disrupted and the subject finds it difficult or impossible to visualize the mental image being asked for. So when you tackle, for instance, Question 9 below and are visualizing yourself inside the box looking at one of the faces, bear in mind that at the back of your brain a set of neurons is being activated to create that mental image, almost as if projecting it onto a screen.

1. If A is on the right of B, C is on the left of B, D is in front of C, and E is in front of B, what is the relationship between D and E?

2. How many triangles are there in this picture?

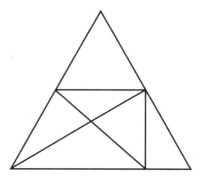

3. If B is on the right of A, C is on the left of B, D is in front of C, and E is in front of B, what is the relationship between D and E?

4. Which is the odd one out?

M   O   A   X   E   W

5. Look at this pattern. Now look at the four options below—which of them is not the same pattern?

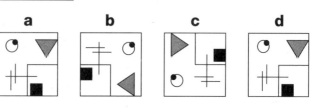

6. If these elements

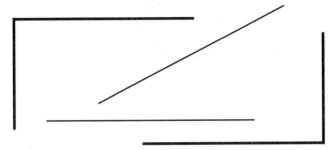

combine to give:

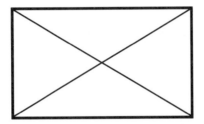

Then what do these elements combine to give?

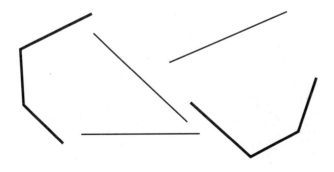

7. You can't see the other three faces of this cube, but you know that one of them has spots, one of them is black, and the other one has a criss-cross pattern. You also know that the spotted side shares an edge with the stripey side but not with the gray side, and that the black side shares an edge with the white side.

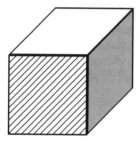

Which of these three is not a view of the cube described above?

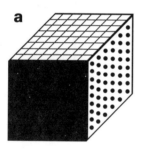

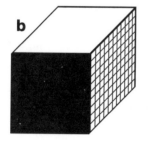

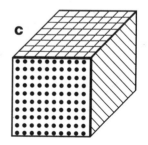

8. You've been left three pots of paint—green, blue, and purple—and instructions to paint all six inner surfaces of a square room, but your instructions are rather cryptic. They say you should paint two of the surfaces green, but that these two surfaces should not share an edge. They also say you should paint the wall with the window in it the same color as the wall to the left as you face the window. The wall opposite this should be the same color as the wall with the door, that is opposite the wall with the window. If the wall to the left as you face the door is blue, what colors are the other walls?

9. Imagine you're inside this box. The other three faces are decorated with a square, a star and a triangle. The face with the square shares an edge with the face with the heart. The face with the triangle shares an edge with the face with the cross and the face with the circle. The face with the star shares an edge with the face with the heart. If you are facing the heart, what symbol is on the face behind you?

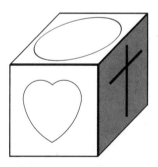

10. Imagine you're looking at a clock. The minute hand starts at a quarter past the hour and then rotates 135 degrees anticlockwise. Then it rotates 270 degrees clockwise. Then it ticks normally for half an hour. How many minutes past the hour is it now?

CHAPTER 6
LOGICAL APTITUDE

Logical thought involves reasoning, making deductions and inferences, and avoiding logical pitfalls. Often considered the "highest" form of thought, logical thinking usually conjures up notions of plotting chess moves, pondering philosophical questions, and struggling through forests of arcane symbols about "if not p then $q > z$" and suchlike. In fact logical thinking is essential to all of these tasks/skills, but it is also much more mundane and universal. To some extent, any thought process that involves either predicting the future in some way (what someone is likely to say about something; what's on TV next; what you'll find at the supermarket); or following rules or structures in some way (playing a game, working out a sum, figuring out how to set the video) relies on logical thought.

However, it also seems to be true that many aspects of logical thinking need to be learned like any other skill. The exact degree to which logical thinking is innate and available to everyone—in other words, the natural degree of logical aptitude that someone possesses—is the topic of much debate and research.

Heuristics

Some psychology research suggests that Joe Public is actually quite bad at logical thinking, and that most people rush headlong into logical pitfalls or errors of thinking, known as fallacies. There is even a long list of common fallacies with names such as "the gambler's fallacy" (see page 167) or "begging the question." This research says that instead of adhering to rigid logical rules, people use mental rules of thumb, technically known as heuristics.

Led astray

For instance, the "heuristic of availability" is a mental rule of thumb that basically says "use the most available information when making a judgement," where "most available" generally means easiest to remember. If you're trying to decide where to find your next meal this heuristic probably saves time (look in the place where you usually find food), which illustrates how and why evolution probably favored the development of heuristics.

But mental rules like this can easily lead us astray. Another common heuristic is the "heuristic of representativeness," that is a tendency to generalize from the particular and particularize from the general. For our Stone Age ancestors, this heuristic might have been useful in predicting the movement of prey animals, or which plants to avoid without trying them all. Today, however, this heuristic is sometimes blamed for our tendency to be over-impressed by the occasional success of fortune-tellers and palm readers—for example, "If she was right about the scar on my knee, all her other predictions must be right and, therefore, she must be psychic."

Folk logic

So are we really hopelessly illogical? Some psychologists argue that folk logic—the level of logic employed by Joe Public on a day-to-day basis—is probably more useful than laboratory studies suggest, and that getting the right answers from people is a matter of presentation. Present logical puzzles that are unusual and counter-intuitive in language that is obscure, unfamiliar, or misleading, and people will fail to solve them. Present them with puzzles that test the same logical principles but do so in a way that makes sense in terms of their day-to-day experience and everyday language, and people will prove to be much more successful.

Boost your logical aptitude

Whatever the ins and outs of folk logic, there is little doubt that logical aptitude is one cognitive quality where your performance can be improved through practice. By practicing a range of logical tests, teasers, and exercises, you can familiarize yourself with basic logical principles, learn to spot and avoid fallacies, and become more comfortable with the language and format of logical questions.

Logic 101

This test checks your grasp of some important logical principles. You should be able to work out the answers even if you have never encountered these principles before—all you need is logic, after all—but in several cases, the right answer is counter-intuitive (which, in itself, seems to back up the contention that our intuition is logically shoddy). The principles involved are briefly explained in the answers to each question (see pages 167–8).

1. If I am wealthier than Martin, Martin is poor. Martin *is* poor. Therefore I am wealthier than Martin. Given the first two statements, is the third one true or false?
2. Blofeld and James Bond are at the roulette table in the Casino Royale. Bond has just won five times in a row by betting on Black. Blofeld challenges him to try again. He obliges with a

smug grin: "Alwaysh bet on black!" "You fool!," cries Blofeld, and puts all his money on Red. Who is most likely to win?

3. If Sandra agrees to date Billy, it will break Troy's heart. Given this, which of the following must be true?

   (a) If Sandra goes out with Troy, his heart won't be broken.

   (b) If Sandra turns Billy down, Troy's heart is safe.

   (c) If Troy's heart is not broken, Sandra has turned Billy down.

   (d) If Troy's heart is broken, Sandra's going out with someone else.

4. Mystic Marge deals four of her special fortune-telling cards (that all have one of the suits on one side and one of a range of symbols and letters on the other side) onto the table in front of you. "Any card with a letter on it is a Heart," she tells you. Using your non-psychic powers, which cards do you need to turn over to check her claim?

5. Every bottle of wine in the Baron's cellar is valuable. How many of the following statements are therefore true?

   (a) If you dine with the Baron and he serves expensive wine, it came from his own cellar.

   (b) If you give the Baron a bottle of priceless Bordeaux he'll put it in his cellar.

   (c) The Baron's vineyards produce only expensive tipple.

   (d) If the Baron serves cheap plonk, it didn't come from his cellar.

6. If Lower Buttlestock is further north than Upper Slubblesmoke, Upper Slubblesmoke is south of High Waistington. High Waistington is north of Upper Slubblesmoke. Is it true to say that Upper Slubblesmoke is south of Lower Buttlestock?

7. If there was never any water on Mars, astronauts will find no sign of life there. Given this, how many of the following statements must be true?

    (a) Astronauts should look for water on Mars if they want to find life.

    (b) If astronauts find fossils on Mars, there must have been water there once.

    (c) If the Mars Global Surveyor satellite finds water, astronauts could find signs of life on the planet.

    (d) If astronauts stumble across Martian footprints, there must be water on the planet.

8. Last week someone scooped the mega-jackpot in the Euro-zillions Lotto, using the numbers 11, 17, 29, 34 and 40. Bob wants to play the same numbers this week, but Carol wants to play 1, 2, 3, 4 and 5. Ted thinks they're both nuts and insists on choosing his numbers using a highly sophisticated random number generator. Which of them has the best chance of winning this week?

Classical teasers

Logical conundrums and paradoxes have often been presented as little tales or fables. Arguably, this helps to make them more accessible and, therefore, easier to think about—and figure out—than the sorts of question we saw in the last test. The questions here require quite involved thought, that means that they test your working memory, because you have to store a number of "if p, then q" steps in your head. It may help to jot down on a piece of paper the steps, possible solutions, and what you know, given the premises of the question. Also remember to read the question carefully, because all the information you need to know is contained there. Having said that, most of the questions also have a fair amount of verbal padding, so you need to be able to sort the wheat from the chaff.

1. You're on a quest to claim your rightful inheritance and depose the tyrant who banished you as a child. On your way to Ithaca you meet the blind seer Tiresias, who always speaks the truth. "At the next fork, you will meet two men. One of them always lies and the other always tells the truth. You must discover from them which is the safe path, or you will meet your doom. But you are only allowed one question." Sure enough, two grizzled old men await you at the next fork in the road. What should you ask, and of whom?

2. Last Friday, Larry the ultra-logical lecturer threatened his students with a surprise exam. "Next week," he warned them, "I'm going to spring a surprise exam on you." All of the students spend the weekend desperately cramming, except relaxed Roger. "Why aren't you revising?" they ask him. "Don't worry," he replies, "I'll talk to Larry and I can assure you there won't be a surprise exam this week." How can he be so sure, and what is he going to say to Larry?

3. You are the village wise woman and four distraught mothers come to see you bearing four surly looking children. "We left our children asleep under the old willow tree and fairies swapped two of them for changelings, but we don't know which ones." You know that changelings always lie, while village children always tell the truth. When you interrogate the children this is what they tell you:

Child 1: "Child 2 is a liar."
Child 2: "Children 1 and 3 are changelings."
Child 3: "Child 4 is a changeling."
Child 4: "Only Child 2 tells the truth."

Which children do you return to their relieved mothers, and which ones do you cast into the fire so that the fairies will bring back the real ones?

4. King Jebediah has received three boxes of delicious sweetmeats from his devious rival King Afukamen, who has enclosed

the following note: "Dear Son of a Noxious Camel, let this be a test of your much vaunted wisdom—one of these three boxes contains the most fabulous sweetmeats ever to grace a royal table; one contains sweetmeats that look identical but are laced with deadly poison; the third contains a mixture of edible and toxic sweetmeats. I have helpfully labeled them all, but I have put the wrong label on each box! Fail to select the divine sweetmeats and you will be the laughing stock of the Levant; pick the wrong ones and you will die in agony. Ha, ha, ha." Fortunately, Jebediah has the world's greatest food-taster, but the poor fellow can only stand one dose of poison. Which box of sweetmeats should the taster test?

5. You are the proud owner of three talking cats, Felix, Corky, and Tom, one of which always tells the truth and two of which always lie. One of them has stolen your fish supper, and you want to know which one, only you've forgotten which one is the truthful cat. When quizzed, the cats will only tell you:

Felix: "I didn't eat your fish."

Corky: "Tom ate your fish."

Tom: "I didn't eat your fish."

Which cats get a bowl of milk and which one gets a boot to the behind?

Read the question

The last test raised an interesting point about logic questions. Are logic teasers simply irritating trick questions? They may seem that way to many people, but in fact they are testing your ability to follow the exact premises of the question. This is a crucial element of logical reasoning—that you follow the premises and don't make assumptions or leap to conclusions. Here are a few examples:

1. Before Angel Falls was discovered by Jimmy Angel in 1933, what was the highest waterfall in the world?
2. There are six cakes on the table. If you take away four, how many do you have?
3. You've just dragged yourself out of an icy river and you need

to get warm quick. You stagger into a hunting cabin and pull out your (fortunately still dry) matchbox, but there's only one match left. Inside the cabin a log fire has been set, and there's also a storm lamp and a portable camping stove. What should you light first?

4. Duckweed grows so fast that it doubles the area it covers every day. When the ice thaws in your garden pond you notice there's a single duckweed in the middle. Thirty days later, the whole pond is covered. How long did it take for the weed to cover half the pond?

5. Can a man in Minnesota marry his widow's sister?

6. Julie's father had three children. His first child was named April. His second child was named May. What was his third child named?

7. The most valuable stamps in the world are British Guiana Magenta on Black stamps. Which would be worth more, 1857 Magenta on Black stamps or 1856 Magenta on Black stamps?

8. A fly lands on the 12-hour mark on your wall clock, and you watch it crawl in a clockwise direction halfway round the outside of the clock, before turning round and crawling halfway back. What hour mark does the fly end up on?

9. Baron de Courbetin leaves three barrels of fine wine to his faithful servants—two fathers and two sons. They happily took a barrel each home. How is this possible?

10. A 5-foot rope hangs from the bow of a canoe. When the river is at a low level, only 1 foot of the rope is under the water. A storm breaks and the river starts to flood, rising at the rate of 1 foot per minute. How many minutes will it take until half of the rope is underwater?

11. Can a non-veteran living in the Commonwealth be buried in a Commonwealth War Cemetry?

12. Dr Foster sets off from Bristol to Gloucester (approximately 40 miles away) at noon riding a fine horse that travels at 15 miles per hour. Little Miss Muffet sets off from Gloucester to Bristol at the exact same time, but only has a rather shop-worn mule

to carry her at a measly 9 miles per hour. Who will be closer to Gloucester when they meet?

Jemima's drawers

A common question in logic tests, including IQ-style logical-aptitude tests, concerns minimum actions required to fulfill a condition, usually with regards to socks in drawers. This short test shows you three types of this question. Learn how to do them and it will stand you in good stead if you come to do a real logical-aptitude test. Remember that these are questions that test your ability to overcome the usual, but not logical, response or way of working things out. What leads many people astray is a tendency to assume that this is a straightforward arithmetic test when in fact no arithmetic is necessary.

Jemima has a habit of looking for things in disorderly drawers in dark rooms. Can you help her?

1. Jemima's sock drawer contains 20 pairs of black socks and 20 pairs of white socks, but they are all mixed up and the room is pitch black. How many socks does she need to take out of the drawer to be sure of having a matching pair?

2. In Jemima's glove drawer there are 10 pairs of black gloves and 10 pairs of white gloves, but they are all mixed up and the room is pitch black. How many gloves does she need to take out of the drawer to be sure of having a matching pair?

3. In Jemima's stocking drawer there are two dozen pairs of stockings in three colors—brown, navy, and black—in the ratio 3 : 4 : 5. As per usual, she's left the lights off but needs to get a matching pair. How many stockings does she need to take out of the drawer?

Numerical logic

Related to the socks-in-the-drawer type of problem is a class of logic questions involving numbers. Although these necessarily involve a little numerical aptitude, the presence of the numbers is something of a red herring, because the point of each question is to get you to reason in a counter-intuitive fashion—i.e. to not rely on the most obvious approach to the question to find the answer.

1. You have a barrel with a notch in the top. Rainwater collects in the barrel at the rate of 3 inches every night, but during the day 2 inches evaporate. If the barrel starts off empty and is 40 inches deep, how many nights will it take before it overflows?
2. The smooth taste of Laramie notwithstanding, it is impossible to smoke one all the way to the filter—a fifth of a cigarette is always left. Harold the homeless guy collects the butts and uses them to construct new Laramie cigarettes. If he finds 25 Laramie butts on the pavement, how many cigarettes will he be able to smoke?
3. Mario the short-order chef has to put a 1-inch-thick slice of salami on each of the 10 pizzas he's making, but his manager is yelling at him to hurry. If he has a 10-inch-long salami and it takes him 1 second to cut each slice, how quickly can he chop up the salami?
4. I have a three-volume encyclopedia sitting on my bookshelf. Reading from left to right I have Volume 1, Volume 2, and Volume 3. Each book is 5 inches thick—1 inch of which is the thickness of the covers. If a bookworm starts munching through them at page 1 of Volume 1 and stops at the last page of Volume 3, how far has it traveled?
5. I have 55 pence in my pocket, but only two coins. One of them is not a 5 pence piece. What are the coins?

Progressive spatial reasoning

The classic form of logical reasoning question in an IQ test is something like that presented in this test. You are presented with a series of shapes/patterns and you need to work out the principle(s) underlying the progression of the shapes, and then apply that principle to figure out what the next shape in the series is going to be. Although this test involves a visuo-spatial element, and thus engages with your spatial intelligence faculties, it is perhaps more accurate to describe it as a non-verbal logic test.

This is a crucial distinction, since one of the flaws in many tests of intelligence/aptitude is that they depend on your ability to understand and work with words and language. As we saw in the last chapter, some psychologists think that this discriminates against people who are strong in the spatial intelligence department (that may even to some extent be mutually exclusive with a high degree of verbal intelligence). It also means, according to many critics of IQ-style testing, that such tests are culturally biased against those who, for reasons of class, education, or cultural/ethnic background use language differently than the people who composed the tests. Research shows that questions like these not only avoid cultural bias—they are also the purest test of fluid intelligence and the *g* factor that it is possible to come up with.

To answer them you need to be flexible in your thinking, since the type of rule governing one progression (for example, degree of rotation) may not apply to the next question (where the rule might be to do with relative movement of shaded elements, for instance). Some elements of the shapes in each question may be of no significance; others may symbolize some sort of instruction that governs the progression. You will need to be on your mental toes to get all of these.

1. What is the next in the series?

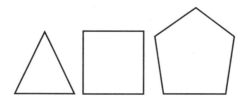

2. What is the next in the series?

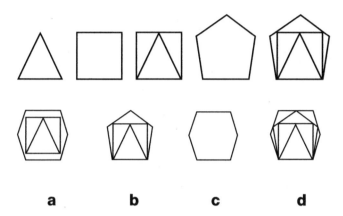

a   **b**   **c**   **d**

3. What is the next in the series?

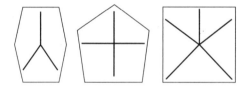

4. What is the next in the series?

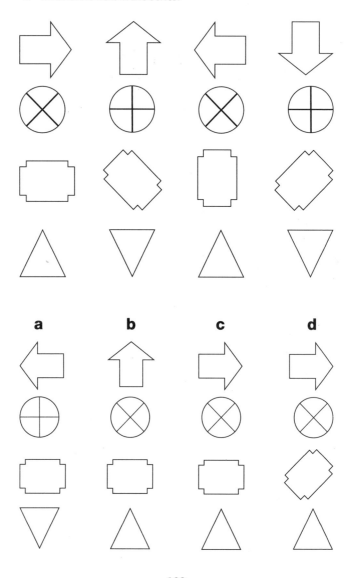

5. What should be inside the last box?

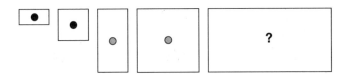

6. What is next in the series?

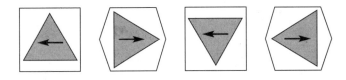

a   **b**   **c**   **d**

7. What shape should surround the last box?

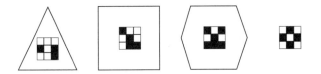

8. Which is the next in this series?

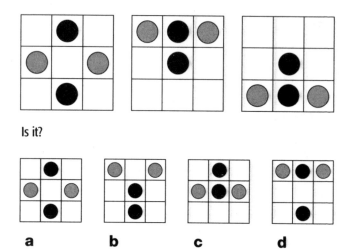

Is it?

9. Which is the next in this series?

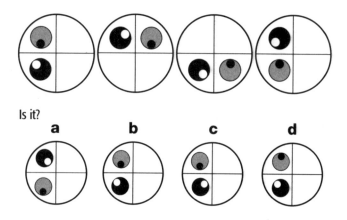

Is it?

10. What is the next shape in this series?

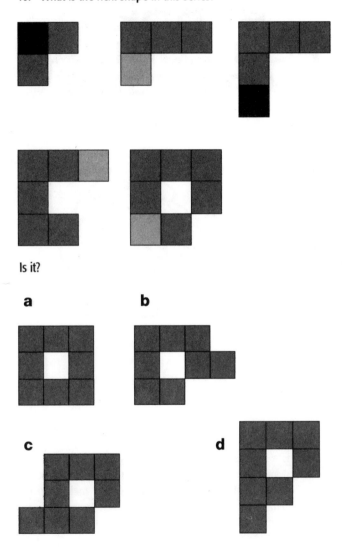

Is it?

a

b

c

d

CHAPTER 7
SUDOKU
FOR LOGICAL
APTITUDE

Sudoku is a number-placement puzzle originally called *Number Place* and invented by an American, Howard Garns, in 1979. It is based on the "Latin square" of 18th-century mathematician Leonard Euler. Sudoku was popular in Japan from 1986 and became an international phenomenon in 2005 on the back of its adoption by British newspapers.

How to play

Sudoku is short for *suuji wa dokushin ni kagiru*, "the digits must remain single," which although an awkward mouthful pithily describes the puzzle. The aim is to fill in a 9 x 9 grid of 81 cells, sub-divided into 3 x 3 subgrids, aka sectors, regions, or blocks, with the numbers 1–9, such that each digit appears only once in each column, row, and sector. Some of the cells are filled in to begin with—these are known as clues. Despite the use of numbers, the puzzle involves no arithmetic or numerical reasoning of any sort. Any set of nine symbols could be used, from letters to colors to types of fruit.

All you need is logic

What *is* needed to complete the puzzle is logic, as you seek to work out from the clues provided what the other numbers must be. The constraints of the puzzle allow you to work out, with more or less involved reasoning, what numbers cannot go into a given cell and which ones must, in order for the other cells to be correctly filled. As such, Sudoku is an excellent and accessible means to work out your logical-reasoning faculties and has become a staple element of many "braintenance" programs alongside crosswords and oily fish.

Glossary of terms

To make explanation a little easier, here is a quick rundown of terms associated with a Sudoku puzzle:
- Cell: space that must be filled with one of the numbers 1–9
- Sector: a 3 x 3 nine-*cell* subgrid that must contain all the numbers 1–9 once each; also called a "region" or "block"
- Chute: line of three adjacent *sectors*
- Band: horizontal *chute*
- Stack: vertical *chute*
- Line: row or column
- Clue: *cell* that is filled in to start with; aka "given"
- Candidate: potential *value* of a *cell*
- Value: number that might go in a *cell*

How to solve a Sudoku puzzle

There are two basic steps involved in solving Sudoku: scanning and analysis. The first involves the application of very simple logic.

Scanning

If a number is present in a line it cannot be present in another cell in the same line. If you can rule out enough lines, you can narrow down the location of the number in a sector to just one line, and possibly to a single cell. So you begin the puzzle by scanning the grid on the basis of the clues provided, one numeral at a time, to see if you can thus rule out two of the three columns and two of the three rows in a sector. This is called cross-hatching.

A secondary form of scanning is based on the rule that each column, row, and sector must have all of the numbers 1–9, so by counting those already present you can see which are absent—if it's only one, you know which one it must be.

Cross-hatching and counting are simple and straightforward forms of scanning, and are steps to which you need to return with every cell you fill in, as each completed cell may open up new possibilities for scanning to succeed.

Contingencies

A contingency is a condition limiting the location of a number. The basic contingencies are the fundamental rules of the puzzle. More complicated contingencies arise when you can tell from other completed cells that a particular value must lie within one line within a particular sector—this is known as a "locked candidate." Even if you don't know which cell on that line it goes in, you can use this information as a contingency to rule out the presence of that value on the same line in the other sectors in that chute.

Elimination and matched pairs

When scanning fails to yield any more answers, you need to proceed to the logical-analysis stage. The main type of analysis is elimination, where candidates for a cell are eliminated until only one is left. A key concept in elimination is "matched cells." The most common form of matching is a "matched pair."

A matched pair is two cells where you know which two values must go in the cells but don't know which is which. This allows you to eliminate those values as candidates for the other cells in that sector, column, and row. Such a matched pair is known as "naked pair." A "hidden pair" is a pair where matching allows you to eliminate other candidate values for those two cells. You can also have matched triplets. A related concept is the "hidden single"—which is where a cell has several candidate values, but one of them appears nowhere else on the sector, row, or column, so you know it must be in that cell as it cannot be in any of the others.

After applying elimination principles to fill in more cells, go back to the scanning stage and see if you can now use cross-hatching or counting to work out more values.

Trial and error

The final technique that can be applied in Sudoku is the last resort of the witless: trial-and-error filling-in of cells, where you effectively guess which candidate value goes into a cell and see if that allows you to successfully work out the other cells in the sector, row, or column. In computational terms this is a deeply inelegant "brute force" approach. It involves no logical reasoning. Guess wrong, and you will not only wish you'd filled in the puzzle with a pencil, but you could forget which values you already worked out—based on sound logical grounds—and set yourself back to Square 1.

Sudoku puzzles

The level of difficulty is determined by the degree of contingency and elimination analysis that is required to complete the puzzle. What follows is a selection of Sudoku puzzles, ranging in difficulty. Use them to try out the strategies outlined above. Don't resort to trial and error unless you absolutely have to.

Easy

	2	5	3	6		4		
	3		9	2		5		
				8		7	2	
	1		2					5
				7				
8					9		3	
	7	1		5				
		4		9	2		7	
		2		4	3	6	5	

Moderate

			1		9		8	2
5	9				4			7
		8			7			6
2		7	9		1	5		3
3			2			7		
7			4				2	9
9	2		7		6			

Moderate

1		2	8			4		
9			4					
7	4		5		6		8	
4				7			5	
	2						9	
	1			5				8
	7		2		5		4	6
					1			5
		5			9	2		3

Moderate

	3			1				6
5	7			3				
	2	9	6					
2		5			1	4	9	
			4		9			
	9	4	2			3		7
					7	2	6	
				6			4	1
6				2			3	

Hard

4				9	3		5	
	3	5						
	9			4	5			1
7		4		5				6
1				7		4		3
9			5	6			3	
						8	2	
	4		7	3				5

Hard

					4	7		3
	7				9	4		
		2	1			5		
		7		4				
3	2			5			4	7
				6		1		
		8			7	3		
		3	2				5	
9		4	6					

Very Hard

	8			1				
	9				2			
	2				9	5	6	
3			7	8				
		2				7		
				2	5			4
	4	8	1				5	
			6				1	
				4			3	

Very Hard

	5	1		9			7	
						2		
		3	2	1	7			
1		5			4			7
7			3			8		9
			4	8	9	6		
		6						
	4			6		7	2	

CHAPTER 8
KAKURO FOR LOGIC AND NUMERICAL APTITUDE

In the wake of the extraordinary popularity of Sudoku, British newspapers scrambled to find the Next Big Puzzle they could import from Japan. The perfect candidate was *Kakro*, renamed "Kakuro" for the British market. The alternative and more descriptive name is "Cross-Sums," since the puzzle resembles a crossword but with numbers instead of letters.

How to play Kakuro

A Kakuro puzzle looks much like a crossword grid, but instead of some squares having numbers telling you which clue to look at, the number *is* the clue. Your task is to fill the squares vertically below the clue, or horizontally to the right of the clue, with the numbers 1–9, such that their sum (what you get if you add them together) is equal to the clue, but with each number used only once. For example, if the clue square contained the number 3 in its top right half and the number 4 in its bottom left half, your task would be to fill the squares to the right with numbers adding up to 3 and the squares below with numbers adding up to 4. (The convention in discussing Kakuro is that clue numbers and answer numbers are written as digits and the number of squares available is written out in full. For example, the phrase "32 in seven" means that you have seven squares to fill to add up to 32.)

Logical and numerical thinking

In order to complete a Kakuro puzzle, you need to use logical reasoning, much as with Sudoku. As with Sudoku you can use the constraints imposed by the rules of the puzzle to follow "if, then" logic to work out the value you need to put in any particular square— for example, "*if* the clue is 13 and the numbers already present = 9, *then* the last square must contain a 4."

Kakuro has the added dimension of requiring some numerical thinking, although this should not be overstated. In practice, the only numerical aptitude you need is simple arithmetic, and even this is effectively superseded by the use of fixed combinations (see below). Many people are put off trying Kakuro puzzles because they assume that you need to be a "numerical person" or "someone who can think like that," when the truth is that anyone who can tackle a Sudoku puzzle can master a Kakuro one as well. The advantage of doing both is that (a) you are less likely to get bored with either, and (b) the logical processes involved *are* subtly different, so the effect is equivalent to mental cross-training.

How to solve a Kakuro puzzle

Variants of many of the same techniques that are involved in solving Sudoku also apply to Kakuro.

Fixed combinations

Ostensibly one of the main differences between the two puzzles is that in Sudoku all the lines are nine cells long, so you know that *all* of the numbers 1–9 *must* be present, whereas in Kakuro the lines (known as "runs") can be anywhere from two to nine cells long, making things much less certain. This uncertainty is reduced, however, by the rule that a run must contain each number once only, limiting the number of ways that some of the sums can be reached. In other words, for some combinations of clues and number of squares in a run there are *fixed combinations* of answers.

The most obvious instance of this is that there is only one combination of numbers that can add up to 3–namely, 1 and 2. The same applies to 4, where it is not permitted to have 2 and 2, because of the repetition, leaving 1 and 3 as the only valid combination. The order of the digits, of course, is not fixed and this is up to you to determine.

There are many more fixed combinations in Kakuro, and as they are essential to solving the puzzle, you need to know them. The table shows all the fixed combinations, by number of squares in the run. Committing these to memory would be a tall order, so you should keep this table handy when tackling a puzzle.

Work out combinations for yourself

You might notice that for each length of run up to seven squares long, there are four possible sums. These four consist of the minimum possible number, the minimum possible number + 1, the maximum possible number, and the maximum −1. For example, for a run four squares long, the minimum possible sum is $1 + 2 + 3 + 4 = 10$ and the maximum possible is $6 + 7 + 8 + 9 = 30$, meaning that the other two sums must be 11 and 29. Knowing this principle

Two Squares		Three Squares	
Target Sum	Numbers Used	Target Sum	Numbers Used
3	1, 2	6	1, 2, 3
4	1, 3	7	1, 2, 4
16	7, 9	23	6, 8, 9
17	8, 9	24	7, 8, 9

Four Squares		Five Squares	
Target Sum	Numbers Used	Target Sum	Numbers Used
10	1, 2, 3, 4	15	1, 2, 3, 4, 5
11	1, 2, 3, 5	16	1, 2, 3, 4, 6
29	5, 7, 8, 9	34	4, 6, 7, 8, 9
30	6, 7, 8, 9	35	5, 6, 7, 8, 9

Six Squares		Seven Squares	
Target Sum	Numbers Used	Target Sum	Numbers Used
21	1, 2, 3, 4, 5, 6	28	1, 2, 3, 4, 5, 6, 7
22	1, 2, 3, 4, 5, 7	29	1, 2, 3, 4, 5, 6, 8
38	3, 5, 6, 7, 8, 9	41	2, 4, 5, 6, 7, 8, 9
39	4, 5, 6, 7, 8, 9	42	3, 4, 5, 6, 7, 8, 9

Eight Squares		Nine Squares	
Target Sum	Numbers Used	Target Sum	Numbers Used
36	1, 2, 3, 4, 5, 6, 7, 8	45	1, 2, 3, 4, 5, 6, 7, 8, 9
37	1, 2, 3, 4, 5, 6, 7, 9		
38	1, 2, 3, 4, 5, 6, 8, 9		
39	1, 2, 3, 4, 5, 7, 8, 9		
40	1, 2, 3, 4, 6, 7, 8, 9		
41	1, 2, 3, 5, 6, 7, 8, 9		
42	1, 2, 4, 5, 6, 7, 8, 9		
43	1, 3, 4, 5, 6, 7, 8, 9		
44	2, 3, 4, 5, 6, 7, 8, 9		

means that you can work out whether a clue has a fixed combination answer without having to memorize the table.

Scanning

Kakuro has its own equivalents to the scanning techniques employed in Sudoku:

Cross-referencing

This is roughly equivalent to cross-hatching. It is relevant when you know that a fixed combination applies to two runs that cross. If the two combinations have only one number in common, this must be the value of the square where they cross. For example, if one of the runs is 4 in two, and the other is 7 in three, the only number the two fixed combinations have in common is 1, so the value of the square where the two runs overlap must be 1.

Summing

This is roughly equivalent to counting. If you know the values of all the squares in a run but one, it is simple to work out the remaining value by arithmetic. For example, if the clue is 18 and the values you have add up to 15, the remaining square must be a 3.

As with Sudoku, these scanning techniques should be repeated every time you fill a square to narrow down the range of options for the remaining squares.

Elimination

Also, as with Sudoku, the next stage in analysis after scanning is elimination, where you try to whittle down the possibilities by working out what they cannot be. Similar rules of logic apply. For instance, candidate values are contingent upon the constraints imposed by the rules and by other numbers you already have. Matched pairs are present in the sense that if you have two squares and you know that they must contain two values, you can eliminate those values from the list of candidates for other squares.

Protruding squares

Something that you cannot do in Sudoku, however, is use simple maths to work out the value of a protruding square. The figure below shows what is meant by this—the square marked A is the protruding square. In Kakuro you can work out the value of this protruding square by summing the vertical clues and the horizontal ones. The difference between them *must* be the value of the protruding square. In this instance: $(4 + 3 + 15) - (7 + 10) = 5$, so the value of A = 5.

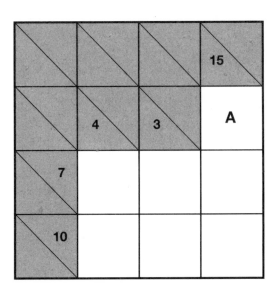

Avoiding duplication

In a true Kakuro puzzle, there is only one possible solution. This means that situations where either of two combinations of values could apply cannot happen which, in turn, means that you can eliminate such combinations from your list of possible candidates. For instance, the combination of numbers in the example below could be the other way round without affecting the solution to the puzzle—each of them would be valid. In a real Kakuro puzzle this cannot happen, so you can eliminate any answer that would give such a combination.

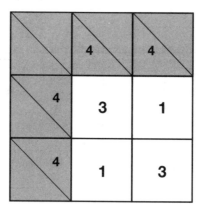

Kakuro puzzles

Below are a number of Kakuro puzzles to give your logical aptitude a workout. They vary in difficulty. The easiest ones can be completed simply by using scanning techniques such as cross-referencing, but the harder they get, the more complex the logical reasoning you need to employ.

Moderate

Moderate

Moderate

Hard

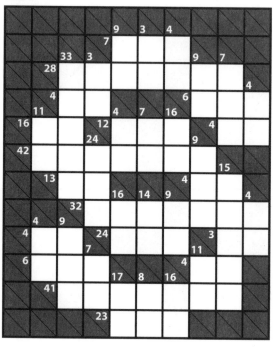

Very Hard

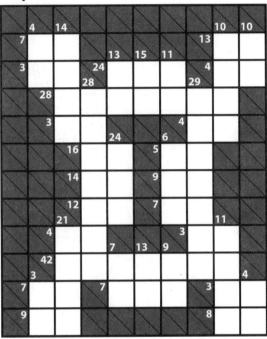

CHAPTER 9
CREATIVE THINKING

Creativity is very much a buzzword these days in business, management studies, and related areas. In an era where mundane, repetitive tasks can be done by computer or machine, and where countries with huge pools of motivated, educated cheap labour are starting to out-compete Western workers, companies and governments are focusing more and more on the value-added element that creative thinking is perceived to bring—the flash of inspiration, the stroke of genius, the spark of innovation.

126

What is creativity?

Creativity is a mental skill or ability that involves ingenuity, insight, originality, and innovation. Creative thinking means, among other things, thinking about things in new ways; coming at problems from unexpected angles; redefining or breaking rules and assumptions; grasping whole problems or concepts as gestalts (see page 35); having insight into the true nature of problems/solutions; and generating a variety of responses to a problem but also having the focus and discernment to recognize useful and/or appropriate ones. Terms related to creative thinking include lateral thinking and divergent (as opposed to convergent) thinking.

Lateral thinking

"Lateral thinking" is a term invented by psychologist Edward de Bono to describe an approach to problem-solving that involves coming at problems "from the side." The usual way to approach a problem is head on, in the most straightforward fashion, as suggested by the parameters of the problem. So, for instance, the way to solve a problem that seems to involve math is to find the calculation that needs to be done; the way to solve a problem with an unruly employee is to discipline him or her; the way to solve a problem caused by inadequate equipment is to spend enough to get adequate equipment.

A lot of the time, this might be the correct approach, but de Bono suggested that coming at the problem from the side could suggest alternative and possibly better ways of solving it. So, for instance, the real solution to the math problem might be to make it spatial by drawing a graph; the solution to the unruly employee problem might be to look at *why* he or she is unhappy; the solution to the inadequate equipment problem might be to find a new way of doing things for which the equipment *is* adequate.

A lateral approach may also save time. Creative or lateral thinking is particularly appropriate when conventional thinking about a problem is not working. You may feel this way about many of the puzzles in this book, especially those in this chapter. You think and think about it but get nowhere. This is a classic scenario in which to employ lateral thinking–changing the way you approach a problem includes changing the way you frame or describe the problem, and doing this can suddenly make the solution clear.

Divergent thinking

Another way of talking about creative thinking is to call it divergent thinking. To understand this, it helps to think about the process of problem-solving in spatial terms. Normally, when faced with a problem, you initially generate a number of possible avenues of exploration and thought–pathways to potential solutions. As you think about the problem further, you whittle down this tree of possibilities until you can focus on one pathway to a potential solution, and then you follow this pathway until it leads to the answer. This way of thinking is known as convergent thinking, because your thought processes converge on a single route to the solution.

A lot of the time, convergent thinking is probably the best and most efficient way to tackle a problem. If it turns out to be a dead end, however, you are stuck–many people find it hard to jog their thinking out of a particular pathway once it's set.

With divergent thinking, you continue to explore multiple branches of the problem-solving process–although not indefinitely, since there must be some rationalization. So, while some pathways to a solution may be dropped, new ones can be opened up. In this fashion, you may arrive at a solution from unexpected angles, just as with lateral thinking (which is really the same thing).

Solving problems creatively

Collected in this chapter are a range of exercises and challenges to get you thinking creatively. They include some classic mind-twisters. The typical response to seeing the answer is to feel that it is obvious in retrospect–in other words, the answers are rarely especially complex or esoteric. So how can you make the cognitive leaps required to solve the problems? Here are a few tips.

Look at how you are framing the problem

Often the main barriers to finding a solution are your own preconceptions/assumptions about the nature of the problem and what the solution *should* look like. Before you can circumvent these, you need to identify them, so think about how you are thinking about the problem. For instance, if the problem seems to involve numbers, ask yourself whether it might actually involve words/letters. If it seems to involve certain restrictions, ask yourself if those restrictions are really imposed by the problem or by yourself. Reframe the problem in different terms and you automatically make it easier to approach differently.

Think prolifically

Try to be divergent in your thinking and to come up with many different pathways to a solution. Most of them will probably be rubbish, but one of them may lead to a flash of insight.

Make new connections

A key marker of the creative thinker is the ability to make original and/or unlikely connections between apparently disparate ideas.

Don't censor

Brainstorming and "blue sky" sessions have an important rule—no idea should be dismissed or ridiculed. This is because concepts of propriety, sense, and plausibility—whether internal (self-imposed) or external (imposed by colleagues)—can force conformity and convergent thinking when the opposite is being sought. Obviously there has to be a filtering process at some point, but initially it helps to remove the shackles from the thinking process.

Sleep on it

There are many anecdotal reports of creative and brilliant solutions to thorny problems coming to people in their sleep, and recent research at the University of Amsterdam has confirmed that giving the unconscious mind time to process information leads to better decision making, especially when the decision is complex and involves many variables.

Creativity workout

The study of creativity—rather horribly christened *creatology* by psychologist Robert Sternberg—is a burgeoning field in psychology today. In particular, scientists are trying to measure creativity, so that they can relate it to other attributes and traits, and perform meaningful research projects on it. It is very hard to measure because of its subjective nature. What seems creative to one person may seem uninspired to another. However, there are several tests that are often used. These also make good tools for exercising your own creativity, and if you run into one of them in an interview or assessment situation, it could help to have practiced and to be familiar with them.

Insert title here

In this exercise, you are presented with the outline of a plot for a story and asked to come up with a title for that story. Your aim is to come up with the most ingenious, original, and/or thought-provoking titles possible, and to come up with as many of them as possible. Witty references, clever wordplay, and original use of quotes and references are all encouraged. So, for instance, if you were presented with a plot outline concerning an ogre who likes to cook and eat princesses, a poor effort might be *The Nasty Ogre*, while a better one might be *The Princess Fried*.

In creatology, this exercise would be timed and then scored by a panel who awarded marks for fluency, that is the quantity of answers, and flexibility, that is the quality (and takes into account the originality, cleverness, and wittiness) of answers. Here, however, you have to judge your own performance, although you could compete with a friend or get someone to judge your answers. Allow yourself 1 hour to complete the whole exercise.

1. Little Marco borrows his mum's correction fluid, only to discover that it has magical properties and can make anything disappear. So armed, he sets out to get rid of school, the neighborhood bully, and broccoli and Brussels sprouts, but learns that too much power is a dangerous thing.

2. Three generations of a family staying in a caravan park find themselves snowed in with only an accordion and an old Super-8 camera to amuse themselves for the week.

3. A colony of termites live happily in an old tree trunk in the middle of the forest until a flash flood carries their home into the river and they find themselves floating out to sea.

4. An army of cyborgs seize control of the UN and declare themselves the new rulers of the planet, prompting a fanatical human rebel group to design and build a spaceship that will carry them to a new world. One of them is a cyborg mole, but they don't know which one.

5. Grenadier Jauzion is a humble foot soldier caught up in the Napoleonic wars. When he finds himself in the vanguard of Napoleon's march on Moscow, he vows to desert and make his way home to his gay lover in Provence, who is himself trapped in a loveless marriage with the daughter of the head of the local town council.

6. When she discovers a human finger bone entwined in wisteria outside her cottage, keen gardener Joan Harden's detective instincts are piqued. As she unpicks the webs of deceit and long-nurtured vendettas that tie together every family in the village, Joan learns that she could be next on the murderer's hit list.

7. A smug lecturer at a top university is shocked to discover that his wife is having affairs with the students, prompting him to examine his own history of philandering and triggering a stark reassessment of his whole life to date.

8. In a parallel universe, Victorian London is the setting for a bizarre revolution as the citizens spontaneously declare themselves to be a communist republic and ban the use of surnames, clothes, and talking loudly. Trapped in Buckingham

Palace, Queen Victoria and a crack unit of Scots Guards must blend in with the populace in order to make their way to Windsor and safety.

9. Two cowboys ride into Roswell at sunset and declare that they have just spotted a strange metallic object falling from the sky. The Sheriff rides out to investigate but is never seen again, and one by one the townspeople start to go crazy. When a US marshal arrives to restore order, he discovers that the truth is far stranger than any fiction.

10. Life on board the good ship *Christmas* seems unremarkable, but the surgeon's diary records the innumerable petty plots and power plays between the crew and passengers as the ship cruises back and forth from Australia to New Zealand.

Common ground

In this exercise, you need to come up with classifications, attributes, qualities, characteristics, or features that two or more of the objects depicted have in common. For instance, the rubber duck and the keyring both share the property of potentially being connected to other things (a key ring to keys; a rubber duck to a plug if it were on a chain). Obviously, there are no right or wrong answers; once again, you are looking for fluency and flexibility. The more objects that are included in or covered by each suggestion, the better. See if you can come up with a quality that they all share or a category into which they all fit.

Unusual uses

This is the classic test of creativity, and simply involves coming up with a variety of alternative uses for everyday objects. Sometimes it is known as "the bucket test" because the object in question is a bucket of water, but it could be anything from a brick to a pair of nail clippers. See if you can come up with 20 alternative uses for the following items:

- umbrella
- garden shed
- towel
- CD case
- mirror
- paper clip
- screw
- cocktail stick
- footbath
- pepper mill

Unexpected consequences

This is in a similar vein to the other exercises, but the aim here is to come up with scenarios for what would happen if an unusual circumstance came to pass. For instance, what would happen if gravity suddenly ceased to operate? A mundane answer might be, "We'd all start floating in mid-air," while a more creative answer might be, "You could get drunk without worrying about cracking open your head on the pavement," or, "If you started to cry, you'd end up with eyes like big goggles of salt water." You're looking for the unexpected consequences—the things that wouldn't normally occur but that would turn out to be significant or amusing.

Here are some other unusual circumstances. Can you come up with 20 unexpected outcomes for each?

- What would happen if someone invented a teleportation device?
- What would happen if cats were intelligent and could talk?
- What would happen if light traveled at walking pace?
- What would happen if people aged in reverse?
- What would happen if sidewalks turned into soup after 11pm?
- What would happen if smoking were good for you?
- What would happen if no one ever died?
- What would happen if weekends came at randomly decided intervals?
- What would happen if it cost 10 million dollars to have a baby?
- What would happen if there was no water on the planet?

Creative thinking puzzles and brainteasers

In this section, you'll find a variety of classic brainteasers, the solutions to which typically require lateral thinking, "thinking out of the box" in some way (see below) or a flash of insight. Remember to examine the way you frame each problem and the assumptions you make about it, and then to challenge those assumptions.

Thinking out of the box

One of the most common phrases used to explain how creative thinking works is the phrase "thinking out of the box." These days, this may be taken to be a reference to the boxes you find in flow-charts/systems diagrams, but originally it was probably a specific reference to the solution to a classic creative-thinking teaser called the "nine-dots problem." This problem is reproduced below, together with its big brother, the "sixteen-dots problem." See if you can figure out how to solve the problem, then turn to the answers section for the solution and a short explanation.

Nine-dot problem
Using only four lines and without taking your pen off the paper, draw a line through all nine of these dots.

Sixteen dot puzzle
Using only six lines, draw a line through all of these dots without taking your pen off the page.

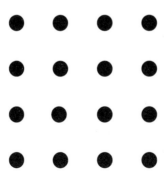

River crossing

A classic creative logic puzzle involves a farmer and a river that needs crossing. Here it is, together with a couple of variations on the theme.

1. A farmer needs to get across a river with his dog, his chicken, and his bag of grain, but his boat is only big enough to carry him and one of the others. Unfortunately, if the chicken and the grain are left alone together, the former will eat the latter, while if the dog and the chicken are left alone together the same thing will happen. How does the farmer get everything safely across?

2. A fox, a snake, and a frog are traveling happily together until they come to a river. There is a floating log they can use to get across, but it only has room for two of them at a time (although all of them are capable of paddling it across). But while they get on fine when all together, if the fox and the snake or the snake and the frog are left alone together for more than a few seconds (even while on the log), carnage will ensue. How can they all get across and remain friends?

3. Santa Claus, Mrs Claus, and two little elves need to use Santa's flying sleigh to get across an icy chasm near the North Pole. All of them can drive the sleigh, but unfortunately both Santa and Mrs Claus are rather "stout," and only one can fit in the sleigh at a time, with no room for anyone else. Both elves can fit in it at the same time. How can they all get across?

Creative problem-solving

This test also involves the creative use of logic, but is particularly characterized by the need to think laterally to solve each puzzle.

1. You are a luckless heretic who has been hauled in front of the Spanish Inquisition. To impress the King, the Grand Inquisitor decrees that God will decide your fate before the entire court. "I will inscribe the words *Guilty* and *Innocent* on two pieces of parchment and place them in this bag, from which the accused shall draw forth one," he declares. "If God guides his hand to draw forth the verdict *Guilty*, he shall be burned at the stake. If *Innocent*, he shall be set free." You know that the Inquisitor is

a nasty piece of work who is determined to hold an execution, and that he has therefore written *Guilty* on *both* pieces of paper! What do you do?

2. You're at the bar with your friend. He takes an empty wine bottle, drops a penny into it and puts the cork in the neck of the bottle. "I challenge you to get this penny out without taking the cork out of the bottle or breaking the glass." How can you do it?

3. A General is riding past an old barn when he stops in amazement. Along one wall of the barn is a series of rings chalked onto the wall as targets for rifle shooting. In front of the barn loafs a small peasant boy, idly jiggling a very old, very shabby rifle. To the General's amazement, the peasant boy has hit every one of the targets in the bull's eye. He is so impressed that someone so small could achieve such a feat of marksmanship with such a poor weapon that he rewards him with a bag of golden guineas before heading on his way. The boy's mother hugs and kisses him before asking with wonder, "Ivan, how did you manage such amazing sharp-shooting with Grandpapa's old rifle? He couldn't hit a cow from five paces away with it." How did Ivan do it?

4. How can a woman marry three men without ever getting divorced, widowed, or legally separated from her husband in any way, all without breaking the law?

5. The Grand Vizier was summoned by the capricious Caliph. "Vizier," he drawled, "I have tired of you and have therefore decided to have you executed. However, in view of your long years of faithful and wise service I have decided to allow you to choose the manner of your death. How do you wish to meet your end?" What should the Vizier say to get out of this pickle?

6. Explain the following conundrum. A man lives on the 12th floor of an apartment building. When he leaves in the morning to go to work he takes the elevator to the ground floor. When he comes back in the evening he gets in the elevator. If there is someone else in the elevator he gets it all the way back to the 12th floor. If there is no one else in the elevator he gets off at the ninth floor and walks the rest of the way up the stairs. What is going on?

Matchstick mysteries

These puzzles have the advantage that you can recreate them at the pub to perplex and confound your friends.

1. Move three matches so that the pattern points the other way.

2. Add exactly 18 matchsticks to make this equation balance.

3. Add one matchstick to make this equation balance.

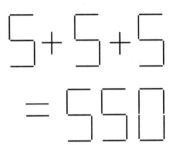

4. Remove eight matches to make two squares that do not touch.

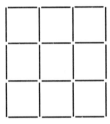

5. Rearrange just two matches to make seven squares.

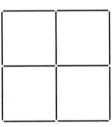

6. Add one matchstick to make this equation balance.

CHAPTER 10
MEMORY TRAINING

Many, if not all, of the mental abilities discussed in this book share a key element—the role of memory. Most higher thought processes depend to some degree on information/input already present in the brain, and the process of accessing this is called memory. More specifically, many problem-solving processes require more than one step or mental operation, and this means that the intermediate steps/operations have to be stored somewhere—which is in your memory. In fact, there is evidence that this latter type of memory, often called working memory to reflect its role, is linked to overall intelligence.

Types of memory

The most popular model of how memory works involves three main stages. First, information arrives, either from the senses or from the mind itself (for example, via the imagination) and is stored very briefly in an ephemeral sensory memory. If conscious attention is focused on the information, it progresses to the stage of short-term or working memory, where it lasts for a few seconds only, unless attention remains focused on it—for instance, through the mechanism of rehearsal.

Working memory
Working memory is sometimes described as the chalkboard of the brain: a conceptual space where thoughts in progress exist, like a mathematician chalking up the intermediate workings of a calculation on a board on her way to arriving at a final answer. In terms of numerical–mathematical thinking, this is particularly appropriate. For instance, when you do mental arithmetic, you store the products of intermediate steps in your working memory so that the subsequent step/operation can be performed on them.

Working-memory capacity and endurance differ from person to person. In general, a working memory that can hold more and lasts for longer helps you to perform complex mental operations faster and better —a long-winded way of saying it makes you more intelligent.

Long-term memory
If material that is held in working memory is sufficiently memorable, that means that you focus attention on it for one reason or another, it may progress to longer-term storage. This may be because you're making a conscious effort to, because it is emotionally loaded in some way or because it connects to other material already in your memory. The information goes through stages of encoding, the process by which a memory is laid down in the brain as a physical trace (in the form of a pattern of

connections between neurons). The stronger the process of encoding, the more permanent the memory will be.

For a memory to be useful, you also need to be able to access it, through the process of recall. The ease and accuracy with which you can recall a memory generally depends on the quality of the initial encoding, so learning to improve initial encoding is the key to improving your long-term memory.

Better coding for life

There are two main theories about how encoding works, and they have similar implications for memory-boosting strategies.

Dual-coding hypothesis

As introduced in Chapter 5, the dual-coding hypothesis says that there are two parallel coding mechanisms. One is based on words and language, and one is based on imagery and spatial thought. For instance, if you have to remember the word "tree," the verbal-coding mechanism operates on the sound of the word, the letters that make it up, and the web of related verbal–linguistic meanings and associations, such as the way you would describe its smell or the sound of the wind in its branches. Meanwhile, the visual-coding mechanism operates on a mental image of the tree, its qualities of form and color and those of related images, such as the way that the leaves looked blowing in the wind, or the image of a branching pattern, as in a family tree.

This dual coding means that when you come to recall something, you simultaneously try to access the verbal and the visual codes. For information that is abstract and may not have an obvious visual coding, such as a smell, or for concepts such as "justice" and "love," encoding and recall become harder. One way around this is to associate even abstract concepts with concrete images (symbols), so that "justice" is symbolized by a pair of scales and "love" by a heart.

Relational-organizational hypothesis

"Relational-organizational hypothesis" is a long-winded term for the hypothesis that coding via imagery does not work in parallel with verbal coding but together with it by placing the verbal material in a visual context. This in turn increases the web of associations and relations between the material to be encoded or remembered and other memories and information. So in the "tree" example above, imagery helps by putting the tree in a wider context—for example, where you were when you saw the tree, what the weather was like, who you were with, and other things that were going on. Recalling the tree would then become much easier because there would be more "ways into" the memory—more conceptual paths via which you could reach it.

Using imagery to boost memory

Both these hypotheses add up to the same thing. Encoding and, therefore, recall are improved by the use of imagery (aka visualization). This applies in both the long and short term. So how should you use imagery?

Make associations
Visualizations are more memorable when they combine to reinforce/suggest each other. If you associate images, recall of one should trigger recall of the other(s).

Be unusual
Striking or jarring images are more memorable than mundane, typical images. For instance, if you need to remember to pick up some eggs at the store, you could visualize a carton of eggs (boring and obvious) or you could visualize a giant chicken in a tutu strutting downtown with egg bombs (unusual and striking).

Be funny
Many of the same elements that make for humor, such as

143

unexpected juxtapositions, also make things memorable and you should try to make this work for you. A humorous image or connection between images is more memorable than an unfunny one. For instance, if you have to remember to pick up nappies at the store you could visualize a large pile of dirty nappies on the pavement (not especially funny), or you could visualize everyone you see out and about wearing no clothes apart from a nappy.

Be clever
In a related fashion, try to be clever in your visualizations and associations. With names, it can help to think of punning associations. Doug might make you think of a man with a spade on his head, while Nina might make you think of an ambulance with its siren on.

Be creative
The advice so far basically adds up to the same thing: be as creative as possible.

Use things you already know
Build on information that is already a solid part of your memory. One way to try to remember a PIN is to associate number pairs with memorable years. If you're going to try this, it is better to use a date that you know—for example, if you were born in 1966 and your PIN was 4566 it would make sense to recall '45 as the end of the Second World War and '66 as your birth year. It would make less sense to try to recall '45 as the year that Roosevelt died and '66 as the year the Beatles released *Revolver*, unless you were a history/music buff.

The method of loci
One of the classic ways of building on information you already know is the mnemonic (memory-boosting) strategy known as the method of *loci*. This involves associating the things you are trying to remember with a sequence of locations with which you are familiar. In medieval times, for instance, religious people might be

intimately familiar with the stops on the Pilgrimage to Jerusalem, and this would be the sequence they used. You might use a tour through the rooms of your house from top to bottom, or landmarks on your route to work. So if you needed to memorize a shopping list, you would associate each item on the list with a location in your well-known sequence. To recall the list, simply go on a mental tour through the sequence of locations, with each one triggering recall of the item you associated with it. For example: milk filling the attic; oil making the steps of the ladder slippery; tomatoes ruining the bedspreads in your bedroom; baked beans filling the bathtub, etc.

Memory-boosting exercises

This section comprises a basic program of simple memory exercises to test and to stretch the limits of your memory and to get you practicing methods such as creative visualization. There are exercises for both working and longer-term memory.

Digit span

One measure of working memory capacity is digit span, or the number of digits you can hold in your working memory. The average digit span is seven (in fact this is the average capacity of working memory for any type of information). Give your working memory a workout by working through the lists of numbers below.

Practicing this exercise (and the following one) could have serious benefits for your working memory and, by extension, for your general intelligence. According to a 2005 study at the Karolinska Institute in Stockholm, Sweden, a program of exercises such as these can actually increase the activity levels of the brain regions involved, and this boost translates into higher IQ scores.

Read each list aloud once, cover up the page and test your recall by writing the numbers down in sequence. How far can you get? Now see how far you can get when you have to recall the sequence in reverse.

Challenge 1
1. 8 3 4 5
2. 7 6 2 4 9
3. 4 8 1 2 6 2
4. 5 3 2 6 3 9 4
5. 1 4 3 7 6 2 6 7
6. 4 5 2 8 7 8 9 3 1
7. 4 7 3 8 9 1 4 8 6 7
8. 2 6 1 9 1 5 3 8 7 4 3
9. 3 1 5 2 7 4 9 6 3 2 9 6

Challenge 2
1. 3 7 1 5
2. 6 1 8 2 7
3. 4 9 7 3 5 1
4. 7 6 3 5 6 1 9
5. 4 2 8 3 4 6 1 7
6. 9 2 6 1 5 8 3 5 4
7. 2 3 2 5 8 1 6 7 9 3
8. 8 4 4 2 5 7 8 3 9 1 6
9. 3 1 6 8 9 4 2 5 6 7 4 1

Letter–number sequencing

Like the digit-span exercise, this is a test of your working memory and is related to your IQ. In this instance, you will need a friend to help you by reading out one of the lists of letters and numbers. Your task is not simply to repeat them, but to sort them in order, with the numbers first. So the sequence "R, M, 8, B, 3, 6, 1, H" would become "1, 3, 6, 8, B, H, M, R." This is much more difficult than simple recall since, in addition to holding the information in your working memory, you have to perform other mental operations on it, such as comparing quantity or going through the alphabet. Work through the sequences and see how far you can get.

1. 4, Z, 7, H
2. T, G, 8, F, 3

3. K, 2, R, 9, 4, W
4. 6, D, A, 1, I, Q, 7
5. 9, H, 8, O, 5, 3, C, S
6. E, P, J, 5, 2, Y, 1, 8, G
7. C, 4, U, M, 6, 3, I, 2, N, 9
8. 2, D, 5, 1, 7, H, Y, L, 4, 6, B
9. G, P, 3, 1, T, 7, S, 6, Z, 9, A, R
10. 8, V, J, 4, E, 3, K, 6, R, G, 7, 5, M

Creative-visualization exercise

As we discussed above, the key to improving your encoding of information and, therefore, your ability to recall it, is to use the power of imagery—the more striking the better. In this exercise, you can practice that skill with a variety of material. The type of material follows a progression, from stuff that should be easier to remember, because it is already visual in form or strongly suggests imagery, to more difficult stuff, such as abstract words and numbers.

For each set of 10 pairs, try to visualize an image that either combines the two items or suggests/leads to recall of the combination. Don't worry too much about accurately recalling the pairs—the purpose of the exercise is to get you visualizing. However, a good way to test the success of your visualization is to attempt to recall the pairings no less than 30 minutes after your initial attempts at encoding. Write down on a piece of paper what the pairs were.

Images

Pair 1

Pair 2

Pair 3

Pair 4

Pair 5

Pair 6

Pair 7

Pair 8

Pair 9

Pair 10

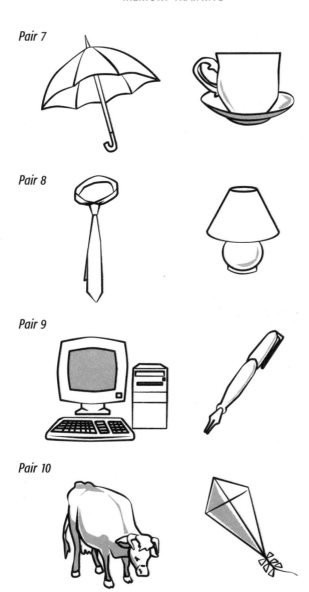

MEMORY TRAINING

Images and words

Pair 1

chopsticks

Pair 2

puppy

Pair 3

cards

Pair 4

wristwatch

Pair 5

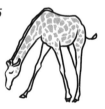

sweater

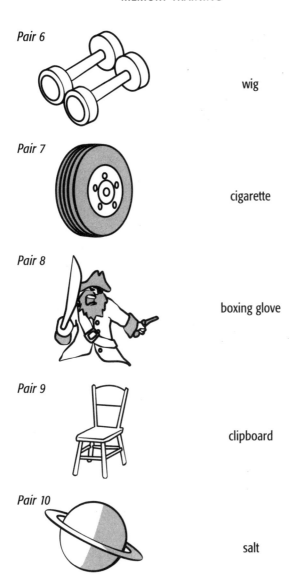

Pair 6

wig

Pair 7

cigarette

Pair 8

boxing glove

Pair 9

clipboard

Pair 10

salt

MEMORY TRAINING

Concrete words

diary	houseplant
table	door
forest	frog
princess	wallet
hair	ice-skates
dagger	star
carpet	microphone
cushion	coal
eraser	slippers
flag	razor

Abstract words

peace	law
love	unfair
nation	sport
duty	pride
clear	yellow
hope	beauty
contain	ugly
dispute	interrogation
grow	heavy
guilt	international

Abstract words and numbers

light	5
line	7
eat	2
busy	9
flight	3
sing	2
youth	6
foreign	1
play	7
anger	4

Name–face combinations

A classic memory problem is forgetting people's names, even after you've been introduced several times. This can be down to lots of things, from lack of attention at the moment of encoding (if you're at a party you might be distracted by the noise and other events) to interference from other information (if you're being introduced to several people at once). Overcoming this problem is a great chance to practice association–visualization methods. When you are introduced to someone, focus all your attention on their name, repeat it to them to check and then, crucially, quickly form an association, ideally with a vivid imagery component. The association could be based on a homonym of their name, a synonym, use of their initials, or a rhyme. Base a visualization on similar grounds.

To help you practice this skill, here is an exercise in which you are presented with a series of faces and their names. Give yourself 60 seconds to commit the first five name–face combinations to memory. Then cover them up and come back to them no less than 30 minutes later. This time, cover up the left-hand column with a piece of paper and see if you can remember the corresponding names. Then commit the next five name–face combinations to memory and do the same thing, but this time try to recall all 10 combinations.

1. Hannah

2. Angus

3. Edward

4. Katie

5. Stuart

6. Karen

7. Rick

8. Justine

9. Susan

10. Dave

Everyday memory feats

At the World Memory Olympics, mnemonicists perform amazing feats of memory such as memorizing the order in which an entire pack of cards was dealt. They accomplish this by the use of mnemonic techniques such as the method of loci. To be able to reliably make so many memorable associations rapidly, on the hoof, is a skill that takes years of practice and probably doesn't appeal to most, but you should seriously consider making mnemonic techniques part of your everyday life. They make for a helpful mental discipline with practical advantages. Try using mnemonic techniques such as creative visualization and association and the method of loci with tasks such as:

- memorizing shopping lists
- remembering people's names and faces
- remembering birthdays of friends and relatives
- memorizing to-do lists
- memorizing PIN numbers, passwords, phone numbers, addresses, etc
- learning trivia
- remembering the plots of books and films
- learning vocabulary

CONCLUSION

If you've worked your way through this whole book your brain should be feeling stretched and a little tired, but all the better for it. Alternatively you may have chosen to dip in and out. If you missed out a chapter because you felt that it wasn't "up your street," you might like to consider going back and having a look at it. As with physical exercise, cross-training is more effective and decreases the likelihood of getting bored and giving up.

Mental exercise for life

The exercises and challenges in this book should be regarded as a starting point for an ongoing program. The long-term challenge is to make mental workouts part of your daily routine. There are lots of ways you can do this. For instance, try to use your mind instead of aids such as calculators, notepads, or dictionaries when it comes to doing mental arithmetic, memorizing shopping lists, remembering phone numbers, or spelling words. Read widely and choose varied topics. Do crosswords, Sudoku, Kakuro, and other types of puzzle.

Play more

Above all, make mental exercise fun. The best way to do this is to engage other people. Games like Scrabble, Balderdash, Cranium, Pictionary, and Trivial Pursuit are specifically designed to exercise the gray matter, but almost any board or card game will do—most involve some degree of strategy, logic, mental speed, forward planning, or verbal/numerical/spatial aptitude. Even the very act of engaging with other people in a proactive, thought-provoking way is good for your mental health in both a cognitive and emotional sense, and has been proved to preserve and even boost mental ability into extreme old age. Remember, we don't stop playing because we get old—we get old because we stop playing.

ANSWERS

3 Verbal aptitude

Anagrams
1. rascal   2. satanic   3. trouble   4. angelic   5. placebo
6. hopeless   7. gullible   8. yachting   9. glorious   10. turnstile
11. inflatable   12. antibiotic

Bridge word challenge 1
1. shelf   2. tooth   3. hedge   4. house   5. fall   6. health
7. safe   8. alarm   9. fighter   10. shift   11. march   12. life
13. frontal   14. leaf   15. fitting   16. mark   17. sugar   18. time
19. band   20. robber

Bridge word challenge 2
1. train   2. art   3. night   4. green   5. it   6. water   7. dog
8. knife   9. story   10. stub   11. spoon   12. dock   13. nation
14. run   15. leap   16. shot   17. ship   18. lock   19. moon   20. gun

Fictional links
1. "Peter Pan" and "Captain Hook"
2. "Beowulf" and "King Arthur"
3. "Robin Hood" and "Little Red Riding Hood"
4. "James Bond" and "Austin Powers"
5. "Indiana Jones" and "Lara Croft"
6. "Oliver Twist" and "Scrooge"
7. "Homer Simpson" and "Mickey Mouse"
8. "Sherlock Holmes" and "Miss Marple"

Synonyms
1. "design" and "intent"
2. "fortune" and "chance"
3. "gentle" and "tractable"

4. "gregarious" and "friendly"
5. "guileless" and "genuine"
6. "paean" and "eulogy"
7. "cadence" and "rhythm"
8. "disturb" and "displace"
9. "innervate" and "invigorate"
10. "last" and "mold"

Antonyms
1. lethargic   2. worthy   3. gelid   4. blatant   5. civil   6. soothe
7. contemporary   8. constrained   9. concealed   10. prolix

Language logic
1. mind: a program is the software that runs on the hardware of the computer, just as mind is the "software" that runs on the "hardware" (aka "wetware") of the brain.
2. rind: skeletons and stones are internal; shells and rinds external.
3. cruiser: an icon is a much grander version of a starlet; a cruiser (a large boat) is a grander version of a launch (a small boat).
4. note: an appointment is something you find written in a diary; a note is something you find written as part of a musical score.
5. oil: rain comes from a cloud (cumulonimbus being a type of cloud), just as oil comes from a reservoir.
6. wheel: a limb is peripheral to a torso, just as a wheel is peripheral to a chassis.
7. teacher: a whetstone counteracts bluntness by sharpening, just as a teacher counteracts ignorance by teaching.
8. vertebrate: comedy is one of the classes of drama; mammal is one of the classes of vertebrates.
9. paper: a headline comes at the start of a (news) story; an abstract comes at the start of a scientific paper.
10. distance: "point" is a unit used to describe the size of a typeface—in other words it's a form of measurement; the stadium was a unit of distance used by the ancient Greeks and Romans. (No one said this would be easy!)

Grid search

1. separated   2. collapsed   3. preparing   4. fortunate

Scrambled synonyms

1.   "cautious" and "guarded"
2.   "beautiful" and "ravishing"
3.   "protective" and "possessive"
4.   "dilapidated" and "disheveled"

Author, Author!

1. Milton   2. Whitman   3. Shakespeare   4. Wordsworth   5. Tolkien
6. Coleridge   7. Longfellow   8. Voltaire   9. Hemingway   10. Nietzsche

Mysteries of English

1.   It is the alphabet arranged by frequency in the English language
2.   They are all collective nouns for groups of animals (pod of whales; unkindness of ravens; parliament of rooks; drove of sheep; bed of oysters).
3.   Each is one letter longer than the one before.
4.   First letters of the numbers 1 to 10.
5.   They all have homonyms—words that sounds the same but are spelt differently and mean something different.
6.   More than half of all English words end in one of these letters.
7.   The word "hole" can follow them all to make new words/phrases.
8.   They are the same in singular and plural forms.

4   Numerical aptitude

Fractions to percentages

1. 20%   2. 300%   3. 66.66%   4. 75%   5. 60%
6. 160%   7. 450%   8. 75%   9. 60%   10. 105%

Logical progression

1.   243 (multiply by 3).
2.   12.5 (each number is 100 divided by 1, 2, 3, etc.).

3. 111 (the figures are 1, 2, 3, etc in base 2. Base 2, aka binary, is a way of counting where the highest value digit you can use is 1, but where the position of the digits tells you their value. In a string of four binary digits, the first digit (the right-hand one) is "units"–1 or 0 in normal base 10; the second is "twos"–a 1 here indicates a 2 in base 10; the third is "fours"–a 1 here indicates a 4 in base 10; and the fourth is "eights." So the number 1011 means, in base 10, one 8, no 4s, one 2 and one unit, which = 11).

4. 13 (add together the previous two–this is the start of the Fibonacci Sequence, a numerical pattern created by the simple rule "add together the previous two numbers in the sequence to arrive at the next," which is found throughout nature).

5. 49 (squares of 2, 3, 4, etc).

6. 13 (prime numbers).

7. 89 (this is the Fibonacci Sequence in reverse, so each number is arrived at by subtracting the two previous numbers).

8. 5040 (multiply by 2, 3, 4, etc).

9. 169 (squares of prime numbers).

10. 36 (subtract 2, add 3, subtract 4, etc).

11. $^{6}/_{30}$ ($^{1}/_{2}$, $^{1}/_{3}$, $^{1}/_{4}$, etc. with the numerator increasing by 1 each time).

12. 10 (minutes past the hour, in increments of 13).

13. 12 (10 x 9, 8 x 7, 6 x 5, etc).

14. 36 and 12 (squares followed by their roots multiplied by two).

15. 34.5 (increases by 3.5, 4, 4.5, etc).

16. 24.5 (squares divided by 2).

17. 250 (there are actually two patterns in parallel, the first increasing from 0 by 50, 100, 200, 400, etc; the second decreasing from 1000 by 50, 100, 200, etc).

18. 37 (add the sum of each of the digits in the preceding number to that number–for example, 11 + 1 + 1 = 13; 13 + 1 + 3=17; etc.).

19. 27 (add 2.2, 3.3, 4.4, etc).

20. 25616248 (starting with the first number in the series, the other numbers are the result of successively multiplying each of these 3 digits by 4, 3 and 2 respectively, so that the 1 becomes 4, then 16, then 64, etc, while the 2 becomes 6, then 18, and so on).

Math grid
Challenge 1

13	21	34
8	1	1
5	3	2

Yes, it's our old friend the Fibonacci Sequence again.

Challenge 2

1	2	3
4	4	8
5	6	11

The numbers along the bottom and right hand sides are the sums of the other squares.

Challenge 3

2	4	6
3	6	9
4	8	12

The top two rows are the 2 and 3 times table, so the bottom row is the 4 times table.

Challenge 4

4	7	2
9	6	5
1	3	8

The missing number is 3— the only digit from 1–9 that's missing

Challenge 5

34	41	46
104	**109**	56
88	80	67

The missing number is 109—starting from the top left and spiraling clockwise each number is the previous number + the sum of the digits of the previous number (for example, 34 + 3 + 4 = 41)

Challenge 6

8	7	12
5	**6**	5
3	1	**7**

The middle row is subtracted from the top row to give the bottom row.

Challenge 7

32	30	26
27	21	13
65	55	**43**

The missing number is 43. The top row sequence is subtract 2, 4, the middle row subtract 6, 8, the bottom one subtract 10, 12.

Challenge 8

2	5	8
7	6	9
12	11	**10**

The squares are 2 + 3, 2 + 4, 2 + 5, etc, encircling the 2 in the top left corner

ANSWERS

Challenge 9

3	5	**15**
7	11	77
13	17	221

The right hand column holds the products of the first 2 columns, which contain the prime numbers in sequence (eg. 3 x 5 =15)

Challenge 10

001	101	1001
010	110	1010
100	1000	**1100**

The missing number is 1100, which is 12 in binary. Each row increases in increments of 4 left to right: 1, 5, 9; 2, 6, 10; 4, 8, 12.

Odd one out

1. 10 x 0.2–all the others equal 0.5
2. 786–in the others each digit is higher than the last
3. $^{21}/_7$ x $^9/_{27}$–all the others make $^3/_4$
4. $^{46}/_{36}$–all the others end at two decimal places
5. 96 + 74–all the others are $n + 0.75n$
6. 8.33–all the others are 100 divided by prime numbers
7. $^{134}/_{28}$–all the others are integers (whole numbers)
8. 422–in the others the sum of the digits is 9
9. 63–all the others are (multiples of 3) + 1
10. 641–in the others, subtracting the second two digits from the first leaves 2

Practical math

1. Combined age of my children three years ago = 32; their combined age in four years = 46; her age in four years = 92; her age now = 88
2. Mungo–his burial plots are twice as big but his yard is four times bigger.

3. Let Rufus' current weight in pound be R, and Max's current weight in pounds be M. We know that R = 3M. We also know that M+56 = (R+56)/2, so 2M+112 = R+56, so R = 2M +56. Thus 2M +56 = 3M and M= 56. Therefore R = 3x56 = 168. Rufus is 168 pounds and Max is 56 pounds

4. Dominic sells flowers in the ratio roses/carnations = 5/8. Therefore if he sells 160 carnations he must sell 160 x (5/8) roses = 100.

5. Total distance to cover = 1.5+0.75+3+2.25 = 7.5 miles. Average speed = 15mph. Therefore time needed to cover 7.5 miles = 30 mins. Midday–30 mins = 11.30am.

6. Ivan made more. Stan's investment: (1,000,000 x 0.6) x 1.6 = 960,000; Ivan's: (1,000,000 x 1.05) x 1.05 = 1,102,500.

7. Speed of train in metres/second = (180 x 1000)/3600 = 50m/s. Therefore length of train = 50 x 4 = 200m. In 15 minutes and 28 seconds it travels 46,400m; so the tunnel is 46,200m long.

8. The first tree was (728 + 54 + 73) / 3 = 285 feet; the second tree was 285–54 = 231 feet; the third tree was 285–73 = 212 feet

9. The average combined score is 212, therefore the total score is twice this = 424. Let P be the score of the Pirates. Wolverines = Pirates = P, Falcons = P+3, Warthogs = P+3-10 = P-7. (P+3) + (P-7) + P + P = 424. 4P = 428. P = 107. Therefore Falcons = 110, Warthogs = 100, Wolverines = 107, Pirates = 107.

10. $60–she bet $15, then Pippa bet $20 and Pam bet $30, then Paula and Pippa bet $15 and $10 respectively to see her, coming to $90.

Box o' numbers

1.

6	**10**	**14**
10	**14**	**18**
14	**18**	**22**

(Add 4 in each direction)

2. 27 (multiples of 4, 6, and 9)

3. 64 (squares, cubes)

4. 9 (top row - middle row = bottom row)

5. 5 (they all add up to 10)

6. 625, 81, and 3 (each row is the square root of the one above)
7. 30 and 7 (the first box has $^3/_4$s, the second box has $^1/_2$s, and the third has $^1/_4$s)
8.

24 24

21 27

18 30

(Left-hand column goes down by 1, 2, 3; right goes up by same)
9. 6, 2, and 3 (reading each box from L-R and T-B, each square is the result of dividing the values in the two previous cells, one by the other)
10. 4—the product of multiplying each column is 100

5 Spatial aptitude

Another brick in the wall

1. 21   2. 22   3. 22   4. 32

Mental rotation

1. C   2. B   3. B   4. A   5. B

Picture completion

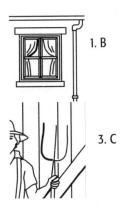

1. B

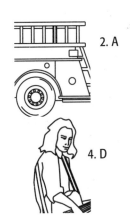

2. A

3. C

4. D

Miscellaneous spatial aptitude test
1. D is on the left of E.
2. Thirteen.
3. D is on the left of E. (This one is much harder to get than Question 1, because the available information allows the formation of two mental models of how the letters sit–in both of them D is to the left of E, but the availability of two models makes it hard to grasp this.
4. E–all the others are symmetrical about their vertical axes–E is symmetrical around its horizontal axis
5. B.
6.

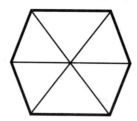

7. B.
8. The floor and ceiling must be green (as we know the other two colors are for surfaces that *do* share an edge). The wall with the window in it and the wall to the left as you face the window are purple. The wall with the door is blue.
9. The triangle.
10. Fifteen minutes past = 90 degrees. So the position of the minute hand is 90 - 135 + 270 + 180 (30 minutes) = 405 degrees. Twelve o'clock is at 360 degrees, so the minute hand is at 45 degrees, that is 7 and a half minutes past the hour.

6 Logical aptitude

Logic 101

1. False. Many people fall into the logical trap of "affirming the consequent." Just because: "If A, then B," it is not automatically true that, "B, therefore A." Martin may be poor, but I may be poorer.

2. They both have exactly the same chance, irrespective of how many times Black has already come up. Believing that prior events can affect a randomly determined future event is known as the gambler's fallacy.

3. (c) This is an example of finding the contrapositive. Any statement in the form "If p, then q" has a contrapositive—i.e. "if not q, then not p." In this case, the contrapositive is (c).

4. The K card and the club card. Most people select the K card and the heart card, which is known as "trying to confirm." In other words people look for examples that confirm the hypothesis, even though in practice the only way to check it is to disprove it by finding examples that don't fit (in this case, the K or the club card). Either of the other two could have anything on the other side, and it wouldn't disprove the hypothesis.

5. Only (d). This is another example of finding the contrapositive. In this instance the initial statement is the same as saying "If a bottle of wine is from the Baron's cellar, then it is valuable," making the contrapositive, "If a bottle of wine is *not* valuable, it is *not* from the Baron's cellar."

6. No. This is another example of affirming the consequent. Just because the second part of the initial statement is true, doesn't mean that the first part is.

7. Only (b). Yes, it's another contrapositive. The initial statement is a negative one (i.e. "If not p, then not q") which means the contrapositive becomes positive ("If q, then p"). Note that the question asks which of the options *must* be true, given the statement, not which might be true. Also note that there is a distinction between water having been present at some point (b) and water still being present (d).

8. They all have an equal chance. Again, this is an example of the potential pitfall of the gambler's fallacy, and a particularly common one. Few people will purposely choose to play the lottery with consecutive numbers or with last week's numbers, although there is no reason why not.

Classical teasers

1. You should ask one of the men (it doesn't matter which), "Which would the other man say is the safe path?" Then you should do the opposite of what he says. This is because the liar will tell you the opposite of what the truthful guy will say, while the truthful guy will tell you what the liar would say, that would itself be a lie.

2. Knowing that Larry is ultra-logical, Roger would point out that he can't wait until Friday to gave the exam, because then the students would know it was going to happen. But this would mean he couldn't wait until Thursday to give it, because the students will expect that (since they know it can't happen on a Friday). This, in turn, would mean that he couldn't wait until Wednesday to give it for the same reason, or Tuesday, which would mean he would have to give it on Monday, and the students will know this which will mean that they will be expecting it. Since Larry is ultra-logical, he can't give a surprise exam if it's not going to be a surprise.

3. Throw Children 2 and 4 into the fire (do *not* try this at home!) and give Children 1 and 3 back to their mothers. Child 4 has effectively admitted he is a liar, even though he does it by telling a lie. This then tells you that Child 2 must be lying, leaving Children 1 and 3 to avoid a fiery fate.

4. The one labeled as containing a mixture of edible and poisonous sweetmeats. Because he knows that each box is incorrectly labeled, King Jebediah can say for sure that the one labeled as a mixture must actually contain only edible *or* only toxic. Once his taster has identified which one the box contains, he will know (because the two other boxes are also mislabeled) which of the other boxes must contain the mixed sweetmeats, and therefore what is in the other one. If the taster determines that the box

marked "Mixed" is actually the poisonous box, the King will know that the other two boxes must be the mixed and the edible ones. Since he knows that the one labeled "Edible" cannot actually be edible (as all the boxes have the wrong labels) it must be the mixed one, leaving the box marked "Toxic" as the edible one.

5. Felix ate the fish. One of Felix/Tom must be telling the truth (because only one cat ate the fish), that means Corky must be one of the liars, that means that he is lying when he says Tom ate it, making Felix the other liar and, therefore, the guilty party.

Read the question

1. Angel Falls was still the highest, irrespective of when it was first seen by a white explorer or anyone else. Note that the question did *not* ask "what was *thought to be* the highest...," even though this is effectively how many people misinterpret it.

2. Four (the question says "You take away four"). This one is mainly nitpicking, but it still makes the point that you shouldn't assume the question means, "Subtract four from six and what are you left with?" if it doesn't actually *say* that.

3. The match. Note that the question does *not* say, "which of the three things in the cabin should you light first."

4. Twenty-nine days. To answer this question you need to work backwards, but you also need to note the vital piece of info: the duckweed doubles in area every day.

5. Of course not—he's dead! We know this because the question talks about his *widow*.

6. Julie. The question tells us that the father only had three children, and that one of them is called Julie. Since we are also told what the other two are called, we know the third must be Julie.

7. One thousand eight hundred and fifty-seven stamps is one more than 1,856 stamps, so would be worth more. OK, this *is* a bit of a trick question but it illustrates the dangers of making assumptions (i.e. that 1856 = a year and not a quantity).

8. Three. According to the question, the fly crawls halfway round the clock (to 6) but then only crawls halfway back (half of the

path it's already traveled, i.e., a quarter of the way round the clock). Some people misinterpret the question to mean that the fly simply retraces its steps, but it does not say this.

9. There are only three of them—a grandfather, a father, and a son/grandson. Thus there are indeed two fathers (the first two) and two sons (the second two).

10. This will never happen because it is tied to the canoe, that floats on top of the water. As the river rises, so does the canoe and the rope with it.

11. He can't be buried because he's not dead!

12. When they meet they will both be at the same spot and will therefore both be the same distance from Gloucester. Where this spot is doesn't matter, rendering the info about times, distance, and speed irrelevant.

Jemima's drawers

1. Three. Even if both of the first two socks she pulls out are different colors, the third one must be the same as one of the two previous ones.

2. Twenty-one. She might pull out 10 black left (or right) gloves and 10 left (or right) white gloves—only with the 21st glove is she guaranteed to have a left and a right of the same color.

3. Four. The ratio is immaterial. This question is the same as the first.

Numerical logic

1. Thirty-eight nights. The knee-jerk reaction might be to say that it fills up at an average of 1 inch per 24 hours, so therefore it will take 40 days to fill up, but this doesn't take account that on the 38th night, having started just 3 inches shy of being full, it will then fill all the way up and start to overflow before evaporation gets a chance to reduce the level back down.

2. Six. He can make five cigarettes from the butts he collected and then use the butts of those to make another one.

3. Nine seconds—it only takes nine cuts to make 10 equal slices. A creative alternative might be to cut the salami into five equal

pieces and then cut them all long ways, requiring just six cuts in all, but this wouldn't give 1-inch-thick slices.

4. Six inches. The first page of Volume 1 is actually to the right as you look at the books on the shelf, while the last page of Volume 3 is to the left, so the bookworm effectively starts just inside the front cover of Volume 1 and eats through that ($\frac{1}{2}$ inch), eats through the whole of Volume 2 (5 inches) and stops just after having eaten through the back cover of Volume 3 (another $\frac{1}{2}$ inch).

5. A 50 pence piece and a 5 pence piece.

Progressive spatial reasoning

1.

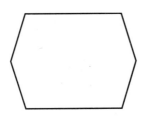

2. C
3.

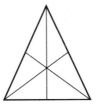

4. C
5. A black dot (to signify downwards expansion)
6. D
7. A square—the number of filled in squares tells you how many sides.
8. A
9. B
10. D. A black square means add one to the right to produce the next shape in the series; a light gray square means add one below to produce the next shape in the series

9 Creative thinking

Thinking out of the box
Nine dots solution:

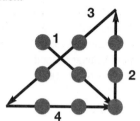

As you can see, the key to the solution is to literally draw *outside the box*. Typically, potential solutions to the problem are limited by the way the problem is automatically framed–the assumption is that the lines must go between dots and only between dots. In fact there is no reason why you can't continue a line beyond the box's boundaries.

An alternative solution is to use a really thick marker pen which is so broad it passes through more than one dot at a time. This may seem like cheating, but it is a classic trait of creative thinkers that they break the rules to achieve results.

Sixteen dots solution:

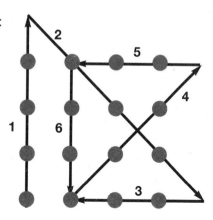

ANSWERS

River crossing

1. The crucial point to grasp with this and both of the other problems is that someone/thing who has crossed over the river can always *come back if necessary*. This is the creative leap that needs to be made, but the natural response to the problem is to assume that crossing must be one way—in this fashion, the mind puts restrictions on its problem-solving ability. Thus, for the first problem, the solution is for the farmer to take the chicken across first, then come back for the dog, then drop off the dog and pick up the chicken and bring it back, swap it for the grain, deliver the grain and finally come back for the chicken.

2. This is basically the same as the previous problem, but where the farmer was needed to power the boat, now all three objects can move themselves. The solution is similar—one or more of the protagonists is initially transferred but then comes back. In this instance, the fox and the frog go across first, then the fox comes back on his own and swaps places on the log with the snake (the problem allows them to be in each other's company for long enough for this), who paddles across and swaps places on the log with the frog, who comes back to pick up the fox.

3. This is a slight variation in that some of the trips must be made with one protagonist only. The conceptual leaps you need to make here are that (a) the elves can be used to ferry the sleigh back and forth, *if* one of them is first dropped off on the other side; and (b) this needs to happen twice. This is how it works: both elves fly across, one of them is dropped off and the other comes back. Being gentlemen, he and Santa allow Mrs Claus to go across first. The elf that was left on the far side then brings the sleigh back and the process starts again: both elves go across, one is dropped off, the other flies back to give the sleigh to Santa, who flies across and swaps with the elf who flies back to pick up his mate.

Creative problem-solving

1. Pull out one of the slips of parchment and instantly swallow it. Then tell the King and assembled courtiers, "Oh mighty ones, I

trust to Divine mercy. Let the Inquisitor show the legend inscribed on the remaining parchment, for then we shall know which verdict I drew and what God has in mind for me." This forces the Inquisitor to show the remaining slip of parchment, upon which is written *Guilty*, so that everyone will assume the one you swallowed must have said *Innocent*.

2. Push the cork all the way into the bottle and then pour out the penny. This way you haven't "taken the cork out of the bottle."

3. He shot the holes in the wall first, and then chalked the circular targets around the holes.

4. If she's a justice of the peace/registrar/vicar she can administer the marriage service to as many men as she likes.

5. He should ask to die of old age and natural causes.

6. The man is very short, and cannot reach the button for the 12th floor. The highest he can reach is the button for the ninth. If there is someone else in the elevator they can press the button for him.

Matchstick mysteries

1.

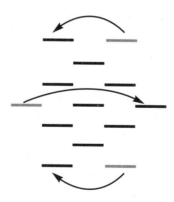

2.

3. Add a matchstick to one of the + signs to make it into 4, to give
   5 + 545 = 550

4.

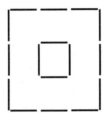

5.

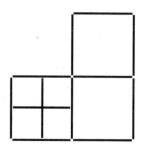

6. Add one to the V to make a square root sign:

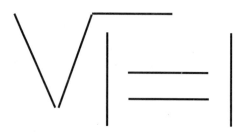